IMPRESSIONS OF
JAPANESE ARCHITECTURE

THE DAI-BUTSU OF KAMAKURA

IMPRESSIONS OF JAPANESE ARCHITECTURE

AND THE ALLIED ARTS

BY

RALPH ADAMS CRAM

F.A.I.A., F.R.G.S., LITT.D., LL.D.

DOVER PUBLICATIONS, INC.
NEW YORK

This Dover edition, first published in 1966, is an
unabridged and corrected republication of the work
published by The Japan Society, New York, and
Marshall Jones Company, Boston, in 1930.

Library of Congress Catalog Card Number: 66-25705

Manufactured in the United States of America
Dover Publications, Inc.
180 Varick Street
New York, N.Y. 10014

To My Wife

In Grateful Acknowledgment of Inspiration, Guidance and Correction

CONTENTS

ILLUSTRATIONS

IMPRESSIONS OF
JAPANESE ARCHITECTURE

INTRODUCTION

It was in January, 1898, that a novel mission called me to Japan. Some years before the flimsy wooden Parliament Houses that had been hastily erected to accommodate the legislative bodies that had come into being with the new Constitution had been destroyed by fire. There had been much talk of a new and permanent structure and at last there seemed to be a chance of the plans reaching fruition. The war with China had reached a victorious conclusion, the Marquis Ito was Premier, and Japan was in a mood for various kinds of expansion, including an architectural demonstration.

A friend of mine, the Reverend Arthur May Knapp, a sort of representative of Unitarianism in Japan, for whom I already had built a pseudo-Japanese house in Fall River, Massachusetts,

conceived the idea of bringing influence to bear
on the Government to induce them to build
something more consonant with Japanese tradition than the dull and very Teutonic banalities
that were prevalent architecturally at the time
and had already been made manifest in certain
tentative designs obtained from resident architects of the German persuasion, " Potsdam
Renaissance " in style and very inferior at that.
The Prime Minister was not averse to the idea,
while of course Baron Kaneko was an enthusias-
tic supporter, and Ernest Fenollosa, at that time
living in Tokio, equally of course. A wild and
wonderful scheme (Plate LIII) was produced in
preparation for the mission and in January,
1898, I set out for Japan, sailing from San Francisco in the little six thousand ton *S.S. Peru,* voy-
aging via Honolulu and reaching Yokohama on
the fourteenth of February.

All went well with the Marquis Ito and his
Government, the idea of a recrudescence, development and adaptation of Japanese secular archi-

I Lord Fuji

tecture was looked on with favour and when, some four months later I sailed for home it was with the promise that an item appropriating twenty thousand yen would appear in the next budget and that I should be authorized to prepare preliminary sketches for new Parliament Houses more or less along the lines already indicated. However, on landing at Vancouver, the first news that caught my eye in scanning a newspaper, was the fall of the Ito ministry, so that was that. Government followed government, the Russian War intervened, Westernization proceeded apace. Ito, Fenollosa, Knapp, Okakura died, Kaneko withdrew from active affairs and when at last the building project was revived recourse was had to the same old European Renaissance, though in the shape of something at least a degree more scholarly than the first German project of years ago.

The original mission failed, but a by-product was the revelation of the wonder of Japanese history, culture and art, one of the results being the

series of papers making up this volume, originally
published in the year 1905 and for long out of
print. It has seemed best to retain them in substantially their original form, barring a few
modifications here and there of statements perhaps a shade excessive in their nature. They were
written under the influence of great and, I still
think, justifiable enthusiasm. The land and the
people were indeed a real revelation: the Spanish-
American War was, so to speak, raging and its
stimulating events gave an added glamour. Indeed, it happened that I was in the Grand Hotel
in Yokohama with my good friend Paymaster
McDonald of the United States Navy — he who
went to his tragic death in the same building so
many years later in the great earthquake —
when the *McCulloch* came in with the news of
the " Battle " of Manila Bay. The various articles were actually written, the most of them,
during the Russo-Japanese War when again my
enthusiasm for Japan was at a high pitch. For all
these reasons it may be that sympathy has col-

oured judgment, but fundamentally I think this latter is sound, not only in respect to the old Japanese culture and art, but in so far as it passes upon the problems of art itself. So far as anticipations and forecasts of both are concerned, it must be admitted that neither has as yet found justification, while the prospect of such an eventuality recedes farther and farther into a dim futurity. As to this point I shall return in the final chapter of this edition, with such revisions of judgment as have been forced by the unexpected and untoward events of the last twenty-five years.

THE GENIUS OF JAPANESE ART

THE title of this chapter is ambitious and perhaps misleading. I have no intention of trying to
express in a few phrases the essence of the esthetic manifestation of a great people, but rather
to call attention to the fact that, in the ultimate
winnowing, the essential residuum is to Occidental hands impalpable. We may look at, and
speak of, and think about the art of Japan, but
we can never reduce it to a chronological list
and a table of formulæ, as is our wont with the
art of our own West.

Somewhere, somewhen, two roads diverged
in the immemorial past, and they struck out
in opposite directions, losing themselves in
the jungle of the unachieved. A race, till then

united, then divided, the half to the east, the half to the west. With every forward step something of the old community of thought and action and aspiration was cast aside. Divine revelation was as diverse as earthly experience, mind and body were moulded in opposite fashion, the last obvious link of kinship snapped, and when at last East and West met suddenly face to face, the mystery of the severed roads that joined again in a perfect ring was no more baffling than were the firmly fixed personalities that were innocent of intention in the round that had brought them together.

For thousands of years both had gone on their separate ways, oblivious, severally satisfied. Somewhere, threading the depths of tangled experience, were others acknowledged as kin: sometimes the paths touched, merged, separated again. There was calling across the wild, interchange of stories of adventure, assistance rendered, combat joined. But these were only threads of the sundered halves of the rope of life eternally divided far back in the shadowy abysm of the long forgotten. The strands stretched east and the strands stretched west, and between East and West was no meeting of any sort whatsoever.

Now the strands have drawn together, East and West; many are lost, broken; some have been knotted again and extended afresh, but where West comes to the meeting with a thick sheaf of gathering threads, East halts at gaze holding a single strand.

This is no strained simile: there is something between Europe and Asia besides a difference of tongues, and explicit comprehension does not follow the mastery of a grammar and a vocabulary. There is an utter antagonism of ideals and methods. Neither can you measure wine with a yardstick, nor Yamatodamashii by *The Data of Ethics*. One standard is inoperative in the case of the other.

In the matter of art, for example, all the tests of detail are different. Velasquez and Korin are

the diverse sides of a shield, either destructive
of other, it would seem at first. And yet going
deeper we find that really not only is either
supplementary of other, but that away down
beneath the lauded and much bepraised show of
each is a fundamental soul that is identical, and
it is this last unresolvable essence that gives eternal quality to both, not the obvious vehicle that
stuns with its palpability, and, to the elegant
rabble, is the " thing-in-itself."

The circling of the world by the streams of
divided life wrought very diverse vestures to
cloak and embellish a final reality that was in
itself immutable. The Japanese and the American, thinking in terms of Nippon and of the
United States, stare, uncomprehensive and mu-
tually repellent, but when either is able to cast
aside the convention race has wrought, understanding is possible, or if not understanding then
at least implicit acceptance.

The trouble is, however, that it is almost impossible to say where racial convention merges

into racial character, and where this in its turn stops before the universal human, the quality that is one in the Japanese and the European. Art is in so large measure a thing of both character and convention, that it is particularly hard for a man to look through and beyond these things and apprehend the ultimate reality. It is hard enough to lay hold of the final truth in religion or the conduct of life when the modes are aloof and forbidding; hard to do justice to character when the intricate weaving is of a warp unheard of, a woof unimaginable; but when art is involved, the task is enormously more difficult.

Art is conventionalized imagination: now when this quality which is so largely the fruit of racial experience develops from an inherited tradition that has been changeless through generations unnumbered; when it grows from a system religious in its origin, now expanded until it envelops every form of physical, mental, and spiritual activity, and this system one that died out of western civilization thousands of years ago, why, the task is arduous indeed.

For all the civilization of Japan, and therefore all the body of her art, is based on a communism that involves the family, the State, and the past, present, and future. Reverence for ancestors, worship of all the dead, recognition of the perfect unimportance of the individual and of the supreme moment of the family, the commune, and the State, — these are the deep-laid foundations of Japanese character. They are far from Western standards, they have made a people as aloof in character, in disposition, in aspiration. All the art of Europe is individual: all the art of the East is communal. With us, the greatest art, the art of the church-builders, the Venetian painters, the German masters of music, is gauged by its departures and its adventures: with them, the men of China and Korea and Japan, the art is greatest that is most conservative, most faithful to reverend tradition. In a way, Greek and Japanese art are closely akin:

each represents the exquisite perfecting in every
minutest detail of a primary conception neither
notably exalted nor highly evolved, yet the result
is, in plain words, final perfection. Byzantium,
Italy, France, Spain, England, each struck out
dazzling flashes of transcendent genius; each was
supreme as a radiant, almost Divine conception,
but none, not even thirteenth century Gothic, nor
fifteenth century Italian painting, was suffered
to develop to its highest possible point: each was
abandoned when hardly more than sketched in,
a new prophet arising to claim universal alle-
giance, and, after a very few centuries, to inherit
implacable oblivion. In Japan one mode, one
civilization, held for more than a thousand years,
essentially changeless and unchanged. Shinto,
Confucianism, Buddhism, all beat and broke
against the adamant of a racial character fixed
for ages eternal. Buddhism did, indeed, create
Japanese civilization and art, but it was only the
Divine spark, the Finger-touch of God, that
stirred the waiting potentiality into activity. As

a religion Buddhism was powerless to bring revolution or fundamental change.

Japan is the vortex of the East. Into her has been drawn the essential elements of India, China, Korea: she stands now, preserved to our own day by the wisdom of Tokugawa Iyeyasu, the sole representative of Asiatic civilization. Her art is not only intrinsically precious, but infinitely valuable as a record of sociological and spiritual development.

I do not mean to imply by what I have said above that it is impossible to judge it by western standards: in so far as these are universal and neither local nor special, Japanese art stands the test as well as that of our own race. Indeed, I am not sure that it may not possess a distinct value in enabling us to discriminate between those standards universally accepted, which are fixed and for all time, and those others, equally accepted, but arbitrary, ephemeral, unsound. All art meets and is judged on one common and indestructible basis: but each manifestation pos-

sesses numberless other qualities, many of them
of almost equal value, but peculiar, intimate, and
personal. These must be judged by other standards, and it is here that I think we shall fail in
our estimate of Japanese art, since the two races
are at present absolutely unable to think in the
same terms. If, failing to apprehend these minor
qualities, we can separate them, and lay them,
for the time, to one side, so revealing the kernel
which contains the very essence of all, we shall be
able, if not to judge Japanese art justly, at least
to realize the position it takes in the body of art
that belongs to mankind as Man.

THE EARLY ARCHITECTURE OF
JAPAN

JAPANESE architecture is undoubtedly less well known and less appreciated than the architecture of any other civilized nation. Not only this, but it is almost universally misjudged, and while we have by degrees come to know and admire the pictorial and industrial arts of Japan, her architecture, which is the root and vehicle of all other modes of art, is passed over with a casual reference to its fantastic quality or a patronizing tribute to the excellence of some of its carved decoration.

Unjust and superficial as is this attitude it is perhaps excusable, for the architecture of Japan being logical, historical, ethnic, is, of course, profoundly Oriental, and it is as difficult for the Western mind to think in terms of the East, as it is for the same mind to understand or appreciate the vast and splendid fabrics of Oriental thought and Oriental civilization.

In nearly every instance those who have written most intelligently of Japan and of her art have shown no rudimentary appreciation of her architecture: it is dismissed with a sentence. To the Western traveler it seems only fanciful and frail, a thing unworthy of study; the shrines of Nikko are assumed to be the highest point attained, and the consummate work of the great period between the seventh and twelfth centuries is ignored. Nikko, Shiba, Ueno, indeed only the temple architecture of the Tokugawa period is considered at all, while Horiuji, Yakushiji and the Ho-o-do of Byodo-in, are completely ignored, and the castle and domestic architecture are treated as non-existent.

This is unjust and absurd: it is as though one presumed to judge the architecture of Italy by the works of the High Renaissance, or that of France by the Flamboyant period; the architec-

ture of the Tokugawa Shogunate has many elements of unique grandeur, while its splendour of
colour and decoration are without parallel, but
it is no more to be compared with that of the
Nara, Kyoto, and Kamakura periods than is the
work of Palladio with the temples of Athens.

As a matter of fact the architecture of Japan
is one of the most perfect examples of steady development and ultimate decay — the whole lasting through twelve centuries — that is anywhere
to be found. In the West a certain style lasts at
most three centuries, when it is superseded by
another of quite different nature, itself doomed
to ultimate extinction: in Japan we see the advent of a style coincident with the civilization of
which it was the artistic manifestation, and then
for twelve hundred years we can watch it develop, little by little, adapting itself always with
the most perfect aptitude to the varying phases
of a great and wonderful civilization, finally becoming extinct (let us hope only temporarily)
after a blaze of superficial glory that led to the

imperiling of national civilization and the submergence of a great and unique nation in the flood of Western mediocrity.

Such a progress as this cannot fail to be interesting to the student of art, while the architecture itself, when once it is known, becomes a thing of extreme beauty, dignity, and nobility, immensely significant, profoundly indicative of the fundamental laws that underlie all great architecture.

Carefully analyzed and faithfully studied, Japanese architecture is seen to be one of the great styles of the world. In no respect is it lacking in those qualities which have made Greek, Medieval, and Early Renaissance architecture immortal: as these differ among themselves, so does the architecture of Japan differ from them, yet with them it remains logical, ethnic, perfect in development.

In one respect it is unique: it is a style developed from the exigencies of wooden construction, and here it stands alone as the most perfect mode

II The Monastery of Horiuji

in wood the world has known. As such it must be judged, and not from the narrow canons of the West that presuppose masonry as the only building material. Again, it is the architecture of Buddhism, and it must be read in the light of this mystic and wonderful system. Finally, it is the art of the Orient, taking form and nature from Eastern civilization, vitalized by the " Soul of the East," the artistic manifestation of the religion of meditation, of spiritual enlightenment, of release from illusion. It is separated from the art of the Western religion of action, of elaborate ethical systems, of practicality, by the diameter of being.

Bearing these things in mind, let us consider historically and critically the beginnings and subsequent development of Japanese architecture.

Previous to the reign of the Empress Suiko in the latter part of the sixth century, Japan was a comparatively barbarous State, but the mixture of Tartar and Malay blood had resulted in a race that was waiting only for the impulse that should start it on its career of greatness. The ethnic religion was a primitive cult of the dead of which the modern Shinto is a somewhat artificial restoration. It was impotent of the highest spiritual good, and when the revelation of Buddhism burst on the people of Japan, an entire race rose suddenly into splendid action. Buddhist priests and monks came from Korea to the waiting nation, and with them, at the instigation of Prince Shotoku, came architects, sculptors, and scholars. Nara became the capital: in a few years the monastery of Horiuji was built by Korean architects, and of this first great work of art on Japanese soil, the Kondo, Go-ju-to, and Azeku-no-mon still stand, priceless records of the birth of a great nation. (Plate II.)

In style they are purely Korean, or rather Chinese, of the T'ang dynasty, for the civilization of Korea was that of Chinese Buddhism, and it is doubtful if any material change had taken place in its acquired architecture, though a distinct refinement was visible in the great school of

III THE PAGODA OF HORIUJI

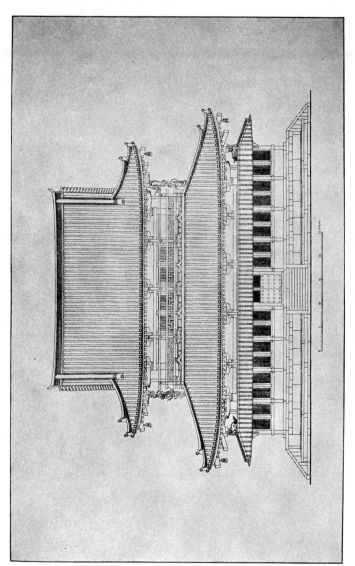

IV The Kondo, Horiuji, Elevation

Korean sculpture that was now to make possible in Japan plastic art of the most notable and supreme type.

This Korean or Chinese architecture was, at the time of its advent in Japan, a style that was almost perfectly developed; in simplicity and directness of construction, in subtlety and rhythm of line, in dignity of massing, in perfection of proportion and in gravity and solemnity of composition, it shows all the evidences of a supreme civilization; as must indeed have been the case, for at this time, the last quarter of the sixth century, China was, without doubt, the most perfectly developed and most nobly civilized of the then existing nations of the earth.

This group of buildings — gate, temple, and pagoda — is the most precious architectural monument in Japan, indeed in all Asia, for it not only marks the birth of Japan as a civilized power, but from it we can reconstruct the architecture of China, now swept out of existence and only a memory. And its artistic value is no less;

small as they are, these buildings are almost un-
equaled in Japan for absolute beauty, and they
have remained the type from which all the architecture of the nation has developed.

The Azeku-no-mon, or Middle Gate, remains
as it was first built: the lower galleries of the
Kondo and Go-ju-to (Plates III and IV) date
only from the sixteenth or seventeenth centuries
and grievously injure the proportions of the
ancient buildings, while the angle supports of the
upper roof of the Kondo are of the Tokugawa
period, and are also unfortunate. In spite of these
additions the extraordinary grace and refinement
of the work compel the most profound admiration; and at first it seems as though there were
nothing more for Japan to do in the line of development, so perfect seems this architecture borrowed from China and Korea: yet further development was possible as we shall see later.

Here at Horiuji the technical details are almost beyond criticism. The plan of the Kondo is
of the simplest type: a central space open to the

cornice and covered by a ceiling of wooden beams, flat, except for a delicate coving at the sides. The clerestory — if it may be called so, since it is without windows — is supported by cylindrical columns of wood; the whole is surrounded by an aisle with a sloping roof. Everything is absolutely constructional, and such ornament as there is, is only applied to the constructive details. The columns have a delicate entasis and the spacing is most refined; the bracketing is straightforward and constructional; the distribution of wood and plaster carefully studied, the vertical and lateral proportions, and the curves of the roofs and ridges are consummate in their delicacy; the colour is of the simplest, — dull but luminous red for all the woodwork, the plaster being white, the roofs of green-gray tiles. (Plate IV.)

These three buildings form but a small part of the enormous monastery of Horiuji, but they are the only ones that unquestionably date from the beginning of Japanese civilization. The whole forms a good model of the early Buddhist monastery, with its central group of temple, pagoda, and lecture-hall standing in the midst of a vast, covered kwairo or cloister entered through the great two-story gate, its subordinate shrines, temples, and halls, and its adjoining street of houses for the priests and monks. Apparently the style of the original work has been most carefully followed in all the rebuilding, and though the cloisters, and all the subordinate buildings, are only a few hundred years old, they are, in all probability, perfectly reliable models of the early Korean work. The general plan is noble and dignified, and the grouping and composition consummately delicate, though everything is on a much smaller scale than in many of the more recent monasteries around Kyoto. The temples contain treasures of sculpture that cannot be equaled elsewhere in Japan, while the Kondo shows on its walls remains of most extraordinary mural painting that make clear the curious combination of influences that governed

V Yakushiji Pagoda

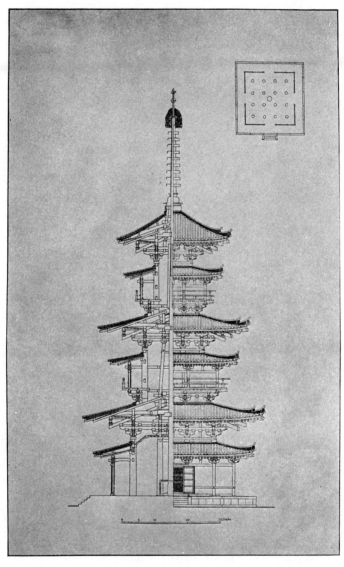

VI Section and Elevation of Pagoda Yakushiji

the art of China and Korea in the seventh century. This is much more evident in the sculpture of the sixth and seventh centuries than in any other form of art, but these singular wall decorations show plainly the powerful influence of India, and even that of the decadent classic of Asia Minor; the only absolute trace of this latter quality as it was shown in architecture is the entasis of the columns of the great gate, used here, I believe, for the first and only time.

Next in date to the work in Horiuji is the San-ju-to, or three-storied pagoda of Hokiji, not far from Horiuji, and dating from the year 646. In detail this very beautiful little structure is identical with those at Horiuji, and must either have been built by Korean architects, or (more probably) Japanese, who dared not vary an hair's breadth from the perfect model. The vertical dimensions are a little greater in proportion to the width than at Horiuji, and as this is directly in line with the future development of the style, it seems quite possible that this is the work of Japanese architects, and if so the first existing instance in the country. At the ruined temple of Horenji, also close at hand, is another three-storied pagoda, the vertical proportions of which are still more drawn out, with yet greater lightness of effect.

Still nearer the present shrunken city of Nara lies the temple of Yakushiji, and here we find a pagoda that is not only unique, but, as well, one of the most beautiful structures in Japan, and also the first undoubted work by a native architect. (Plate V.) If the prototype of so revolutionary a structure existed in China we can never know, but as this triumph of imagination dates from the year 680, a full century after the coming of the Korean architects, and as it is full of characteristically Japanese features, we are, I think, justified in accrediting it to native genius, particularly as its date corresponds exactly with that of the highest level reached by the first great school of purely Japanese sculpture.

This pagoda of Yakushiji is one of the most daring, original and yet successful works of architecture in Japan; nothing of the delicacy of line, frankness of construction, subtlety of proportion so characteristic of Horiuji is wanting, but in place of the severe and classic masses of the Korean work is an aspiring lightness, a captivating grace that only find a parallel in the medieval architecture of Europe. And yet this consummate achievement was the work of a people separated by hardly more than a century from practical barbarism, and it had already stood five hundred years when Europe emerged from the dark ages and first began her tentative efforts at building a new civilization and a new art.

The pagoda of Yakushiji marks the birth of national Japanese architecture; in it may be discovered the germs of its future development; loftiness and varied grace in place of the sombre severity of the Chinese model, daring originality, richness and elaboration of detail. Here, for the first time, we find the doubled brackets that were

to develop into the splendid system of the Kamakura and Ashikaga periods and ultimately fritter
themselves away in the trivialities of the Tokugawa régime.

From this single example we may form some
idea of the general architecture of the period, but
it can only be inadequate. Owing to the perishable nature of the building material, the constant
wars that ravaged Japan, and the incessant moving of the Court, nearly every work of architecture dating from the first three centuries of Japanese civilization has been destroyed. All the
important temples and all the palaces of the
seventh and eighth centuries that cover the Nara
period are gone, and all that remains is this one
pagoda of a comparatively small temple. Yet at
the close of this period Nara covered an area of
nearly thirty square miles, and had a population
of more than half a million. Hundreds of temples
surrounded it, and the hills were full of monasteries, while the Imperial palace, fashioned probably after the gorgeous palaces of China, must

have been a structure of extreme beauty. Of this latter no tradition — I believe — remains, but judging from the slight changes that took place in temple architecture between the Tenchi and Fujiwara periods, we are justified in finding some hint of its nature in one building that dates from the eleventh century, the Ho-o-do of the temple of Byodo-in at Uji.

Before this wonderful building was erected, Japanese architecture had passed through several stages; the first Korean impulse had worked itself out, and from the year 725 on to the beginning of the ninth century there was a steady retrogression both in sculpture and architecture. The only buildings of this period that remain are the small and very simple temples of Toshodaiji, Todaiji and Shinyakushiji, all of which show a primitive plan, simple construction, low roofs, and absence of ornament. With the ninth century came, however, a new impulse, this time directly from China, and at once Japanese civilization leaped to a height unattained before. The Court was removed to what is now Kyoto, and organized on the most elaborate Chinese lines: learning, philosophy, the fine arts, manners, became the objects of study for the new and magnificent aristocracy, and a veritable golden age of culture began. This was the period of the Fujiwara, and the best record of its magnificence now left us is this same Ho-o-do at Uji, now a small village, only a few miles from Kyoto.

No description and no photograph can give any idea of the almost inconceivable grace and dignity of this unique building. (Plates VII and VIII.) It is in the purest palace style and consists of a central shrine approached from the rear by a long, enclosed corridor, and with open two-story arcades terminating in low pavilions, reaching out on either hand. In delicacy of proportion and refinement of composition it marks the culmination of Japanese architecture; the coming centuries were to see structures of far greater size, grandeur, and dramatic quality, but in no instance were they to approach this " Phœnix

VII Ho-o-do, Uji

VIII Sanctuary of the Ho-o-do

Hall " in all that makes for refinement and classical perfection.

Exquisite as this building is from without, one must go inside to learn of the splendid gorgeousness that characterized the work of the Fujiwara period; ruined by neglect and inevitable decay it yet remains beautiful in line, detail, and design. In the days of its glory it must have been a marvel, for all the woodwork of the wonderfully carved and coffered ceiling was covered with black lacquer inlaid with ivory, mother-of-pearl, and silver, while all below was gilding and polychromatic decoration.

These, then, are the three temples from whose few remains we must learn all that we can ever know of the architecture of the first five centuries of Japanese civilization, Horiuji, Yakushiji, and Byodo-in. Carefully studied and without Western prejudice, they will be seen to indicate inevitably the existence in Japan of a system and school of architecture quite worthy to take its place with the already recognized schools of classical, medieval, and Renaissance Europe.

In them one sees at once how unjust must be a judgment of Japanese architecture founded on the shrines of Shiba and Nikko, and the crowded temples of the Tokugawa period that rise in every village in Japan. In every detail the early work has been coarsened and vulgarized; the low roofs with their wonderful curves have risen to gigantic sweeps of blue tile, steep, coarsely curved, and loaded with huge ridges; the bracketing has become a wilderness of tortured carving and joinery, tedious and overloaded: ornament is no longer constructional, it is arbitrary, and by its very prodigality it becomes cheap and tawdry. So far as the interior is concerned, the results have been by no means so bad, for the Korean work was simple — almost forbidding; and it must be confessed that a temple interior, like that of Chion-in at Kyoto, leaves almost no loophole for criticism, while the inconceivable richness of Shiba and Nikko is yet in perfect taste.

The riotousness that occurred in external work never happened to a like degree in the interior, and the plan and details remain simple and closely modeled on the early work. The greatest revolution was in decoration, and instead of the Korean woodwork covered with red oxide of lead, the white plaster and formal wall painting, came an apotheosis of colour. Certain temple interiors are a glory of burnished gold, columns, walls, and ceilings, with just enough black and red lacquer to give the required accent; in others, the black lacquer predominates, and the floors and columns are like polished ebony; in others every inch of the fabric is painted in brilliant yet delicate colours. Whatever the treatment, the effect is always splendid and imposing, sometimes, as at Chion-in, unspeakably sublime, and matched, if matched at all, only by St. Mark's in Venice, or the Cappella Palatina in Palermo. After the time of the Fujiwara, Japanese architecture certainly degenerated steadily, but decoration advanced with equal rapidity until the opening of the ports by Commodore Perry started the final catastrophe that has involved both architecture and decoration, if nothing else, in final, if not irretrievable, ruin.

THE LATER ARCHITECTURE OF
JAPAN

TOWARDS the end of the fourteenth century the
dynasty of Fujiwara Shoguns was finally overthrown after almost two centuries of domestic
warfare, and a new line was established, that of
the Ashikaga, who completely severed themselves from the Imperial Court at Kyoto, and,
building the great city of Kamakura far to the
north and near the site of the present capital,
began a new and brilliant, though corrupt and
chaotic, administration.

During the two centuries of internal conflict
Japan had almost wholly cut herself off from
China, the great source of learning and culture,
but by the founding of the Ashikaga dynasty in-
tercourse was resumed, and under the influence
of the Zen mission temple building began again

on new lines, and a recrudescence of Chinese influence came into existence.

At this time the Ming dynasty was striving to restore the almost incredible glories of that of the Sung which had made Hangchow the culmination of world civilization in the twelfth century. For some years Buddhist priests had been coming from China to Japan bringing the new gospel according to the Zen sect, and now, with peace established, their work began to show its results. A new epoch of civilization, generally called the Kamakura period, set in, and architecture received a new accession of vitality, reaching its last phase of greatness before the first trace of decay showed itself under the Tokugawa Shoguns. Two sets of buildings are most characteristic of this period: the Zen temples and the palace pavilions of Kyoto.

In the former we immediately see certain deviations from the old types. The arrangement of the group of temple buildings is different; there is seldom a pagoda, and the temple and preaching hall stand one behind the other in the centre of the main enclosure; libraries, schoolrooms and monastic buildings surround this space, and oftentimes open cloisters connect them with the central temples, dividing the entire area into three great courts; minor courtyards with shrines and schools and priests' houses continue the group on either hand in complete bilateral symmetry. In many cases the group of buildings is laid out on a vast and imposing plan, but in almost every instance so many of the buildings have been burned that little idea can be gained of the original design. The gigantic monastery of Obaku-san between Uji and Kyoto, though dating from the middle of the seventeenth century, is perhaps the most complete example of the great Zen temple in Japan.

The low and often long temples of the Korean style give place in the Zen architecture to buildings that are nearly square, and very loftly inside. A central space reaches high into the roof, which rests on twelve widely spaced columns, often of great size. One and sometimes two aisles surround this central area, and small shrines, chapels, and altars are grouped at the chancel end. The temple itself is raised on a low stone terrace, and the floor is also of stone slabs. Plaster is seldom used, all the work being of wood, and the roofs rise in steep and graceful curves. The system of bracketing is becoming more and more elaborate and complex, but carving is still almost wholly absent. This is the type of architecture that became fixed in Japan and persevered until the Tokugawa régime, when it burst into such unexampled exuberance and luxury.

Of the palace architecture of this time we have still the fragments at Ginkaku-ji and Kinkaku-ji in Kyoto. As both these delicate little structures were originally but garden pavilions it is possible that they do not exactly represent the more dignified work of the time, but they certainly bear a close resemblance to the Chinese palaces as

IX Kinkakuji, Kyoto

X A Study in Curves

they are recorded for us in the screens painted by the great artists of the age. The grandeur and dignity of the Fujiwara or Kyoto style has given place to a lightness and grace that are very charming. (Plate IX.) Originally one of these pleasure pavilions was entirely covered with gold leaf, the other with silver, and in this gorgeous innovation we find the first indication of the tendency that was to reach its climax under the Tokugawa.

With the end of the sixteenth century came the fall of the Ashikaga, the revolt and triumph of the barons under the adventurer Hideyoshi, and the almost simultaneous founding of the Tokugawa dynasty by Iyeyasu, the establishment of one of the most perfect feudal systems the world has ever known, the transferring of the capital of the Shogun to Yeddo, and the closing of Japan to the outer world. This tremendous revolution was accomplished within a period of thirty-five years, the overthrow of the Ashikaga marking the beginning, the closing of the ports the consummation of the revolution that cut Japan off from the world and held her so for two hundred and twenty-five years.

The epoch which followed was one of industrial development and domestic civilization. The Tokugawa feudalism was one of the most elaborate and perfect of which we have record, and under it Japan was peaceful, prosperous, and happy. One fatal error was made by the founders of the dynasty, otherwise so notably judicious and far seeing. There must be no rival power in the State, and therefore not only was Christianity, at the time numbering hundreds of thousands of converts, utterly destroyed, but Buddhism was violently antagonized, and in its place a revival of Confucianism attempted, an empty system of ethics unvitalized by any religious element. The attempt was successful in a measure, and ultimately led to the blunder of revived Shinto, while Buddhism, out of favour with the nobility and the knighthood, fell back upon the support of the peasantry, with the inevitable results.

As a consequence of this sequence of events, architecture, cut off from Chinese influence, and answering to the demands of the new society with all its ostentatious magnificence, burst into a riot of unparalleled decoration. The development of the industrial arts made possible a degree of splendour hitherto inconceivable, and for the future, until the opening of the ports sounded the death knell of the ancient régime, architecture was to be merged in decoration, losing little by little its original qualities as a system of constructive design.

One curious reaction took place in the shape of a third recrudescence of the Chinese type just at the time of the closing of Japan. Obaku-san near Uji, already referred to, is the great monument of the classical style, and it came as a protest against the almost barbaric richness of the work of Hideyoshi's time. Complete as it is in plan and imposing in design, it is yet weak and inferior in detail, and shows very clearly how self-conscious and affected an imitation it was of the Chinese type.

This last flicker of classical influence was purely sporadic, and quite impotent to stop the triumphant progress of the luxurious style already formulating itself at Nikko in the shrine of Iyeyasu. (Plates XI and XII.)

In the presence of this bewildering piece of reckless ornamentation one is apt to be blinded by its extravagance to the actual shortcomings of its architecture; but once strip it of its carving, its lacquer, its gold leaf and polychromatic decoration, and compare it in detail with the work of the Korean period, or even of the Fujiwara and Ashikaga, and it is easy to see how great has been the fall: the roofs are heavy and often coarse in their curves, the roof ridges and ribs have become enormous, crude, and meaningless, the bracketing is fantastic and irrational in its intricacy and has lost the last structural excuse. Above all, the following of the lines, the curve

XI Nikko Gate

XII An Interior, Nikko

composition, is no longer inevitably good. In the work of the Nara and Kyoto period one may view a building from any point, and by some magical power the architect has so composed his curves that there is not a discord, a lack of rhythm anywhere. (See Plate X.) Under the Tokugawa this is no longer true, and one is constantly shocked at some violent discord in the composition of line.

It is quite true that many of the temples of this period, like the Higashi Hongwanji at Nagoya, are tremendously imposing — more so in size and general effect than any of the earlier structures — and occasionally there is almost no fault to be found with the composition of their curves; but too often size is the only reason for admiration.

Leave out the question of pure architecture and the Nikko shrines, together with those of Shiba and Uyeno in Tokyo, are marvels of exquisite art. The decoration is masterly, the dramatic and pictorial effect triumphant, but it is the triumph of prodigal decoration, not of architectural achievement.

Throughout Japan the majority of temples that now exist date from this period of the Tokugawa Shogunate. None of them approaches the gorgeousness of Nikko, Shiba, and Uyeno, but many are vastly greater and more dignified. In all of them, however, one can trace the progressive coarsening of detail and loss of sense of perfect curvature, until they reach the final point of degradation in the contemporary Shinto shrine, Shokonsha, and the main temple of the monastery of Zojoji, both in Tokyo. Internally the Tokugawa temples are less susceptible of adverse criticism, many of them, like Chion-in and Nishi Hongwanji in Kyoto, being models of religious grandeur and solemn splendour. In this respect, as examples of interior decoration, the Nikko shrines and those at Shiba may be placed beyond criticism. Every period in Japan has had its fitting artistic expression, sculpture, architecture, religious, historic, and genre painting, and decoration, and the last is the true manifestation of the Tokugawa Shogunate.

Of the secular architecture of this period we have many existing examples, all, as was to be expected, characteristic of the dominant feudalism. The great castles of Himeiji, Kumamoto, Nagoya, and Hikone are magnificent representations of the feudal establishments of the daimyo, or territorial nobles, and it is most regrettable that their palaces in Tokyo, where they were compelled to live a portion of the year, have been destroyed, nothing remaining but the great gates and surrounding barracks. The arrangement of these " yashiki " varied but little: a hollow square, often very large, was formed by the barracks for the daimyo's retainers; these barracks were usually two stories in height, surmounted by low pitched roofs of tiles with the heavy ridges and angle rolls with their clumsy terminals so characteristic of the last stages of Japanese architecture; the walls were covered with black or blue-gray tiles, about eighteen inches square, set diagonally, the joints being protected by great rolls of cement. In the centre of the principal façade was the great gate, used only by the daimyo or by guests of equal station; these gates were the most elaborate and stately portions of the entire group of buildings, and are of two types: the first a single line of gigantic columns of wood, square, and capped and bound with bronze or iron, supporting a massive system of huge beams that bore the tiled roof. On either side were porters' lodges and rooms for the guard, usually very rich in design and forming a part of the whole composition. (Plate XIII.) The second type was one which took the place of that already described, in case it should have been destroyed by fire; because of some superstition or prejudice, the original gate could never be restored on the same lines. These substitute gates still retained the flanking guard-houses, but the main roof was omitted, and the enormous posts with the equally massive cross-bar acted no longer as supports, except for the pon-

XIII A YASHIKI GATE

XIV The Royal Palace, Kyoto

derous gates, studded with big bronze bolt-heads.

Inside the quadrangle of barracks came a second for the accommodation of the domestic officials of the household, and finally in the centre of all was the daimyo's yashiki, a plain one-story building, huge in extent, but very simple. A forest of square wooden columns arranged on a unit of six feet formed the frame of the structure, and sliding screens of rice-paper or heavy wooden " fusuma," gorgeously painted and gilded, filled in the spaces between the posts, forming rooms of various sizes. In certain specified places the walls were of solid plaster, but this was unusual except around the place of honour where were the two alcoves called " tokonoma " and " chigai-dana," in the chief rooms. Around the greater part of the house was a narrow gallery, called the " yen-gawa," which by its projecting roof served to protect the rice-paper screens, or shoji, that formed the outer walls of the house. The principal rooms, " jo-dan " and " ge-dan," were often of great size; the former was raised a step above the latter, and at the end were the tokonoma and chigai-dana where the picture for the day, and a choice selection from the art treasures of the daimyo, were exposed. On one side of the upper room where the lord sat on state occasions were two doors of the most gorgeous workmanship, through which he came from his anteroom. Around these two rooms ran the iri-kawa, or corridor, from six to nine feet wide, forming in fact a portion of the state apartments, though of less honour than the jo-dan.

In the Japanese house there is no distinction between parlour, dining-room, and bedroom, so a repetition of the group of rooms already described, together with reception-rooms, kitchens, baths, and rooms for the taking of tea, made up the entire yashiki.

The royal palaces are extremely simple and monastic (see Plate XIV), but within the decoration is often splendid beyond description; gold, black lacquer, carved wood, coved and coffered ceilings, and splendid wall paintings making up a whole of extraordinary richness; but in the palace of the daimyo much greater simplicity was the rule, and the wood was usually left with a natural satiny surface, while the ceilings were of plain boards delicately veined and coloured, the whole effect being one of great simplicity, reserve, and refinement.

In the country castles of the nobles there was a still greater degree of simplicity, the daimyo usually having near by a more domestic dwelling on the lines of the Tokyo yashiki, the castle being principally for refuge in case of attack. Many of the castles still remain in an almost complete condition, Himeiji in particular being a most noble structure. If the site were level, vast walls of stone curved upward from a wide moat, crowned by tiled and plastered paraphets. Extensive barracks stood within, and in the midst rose the great keep, three or five stories in height, each story somewhat smaller than the one below, the roofs curving outward in noble lines. These keeps were built of enormous timbers, the walls being filled in several feet thick with wattles and clay and covered outside with fine white plaster. Sometimes they were plain and ungraceful like Nagoya, but often they were wonderfully imposing, and withal graceful, like Himeiji, Kumamoto (Plate XV), or better still Hikone (Plate XVI).

I have dwelt at length on the arrangement of the yashiki, for with allowances for the difference in station of the respective owners, it is practically a type of the contemporary domestic architecture of Japan. The system of construction is the same and the arrangement of the rooms very similar, except that the state corridor is often absent and the jo-dan and ge-dan have become modest apartments of eight or ten mats in size, and serve as parlour, bedroom, and dining-room as the case may demand.

It must be evident that where construction is entirely of wood conflagrations must be pretty certain, and such is the case, a fire that does not

XV Kumamoto Castle

XVI HIKONE CASTLE

destroy a thousand houses hardly being considered worthy of chronicling in the daily papers. For the protection of valuables, therefore, a separate and fireproof building is imperative, and every house of any pretension possesses its " kura," or storehouse, built of wood and bamboo, but covered two feet thick with clay that effectually resists a conflagration of the utmost fierceness. After a big fire in a Japanese city, nothing is left but fine ashes and the scorched but reliable kura.

We have now reached the present day, and only a word is necessary as to the architecture under the new régime of Westernism and " progress." Domestic work is still almost wholly on the old lines, so far as the middle classes are concerned: the nobles are building palaces from European designs that would dishonour a trans-Mississippi city or a German suburb. The public buildings designed by local " foreign " architects are even worse, and the least offensive examples of Western styles are the work of natives, the

Nippon Ginko and the Teikoku Hotel [1] being fairly creditable examples of German classic. Occasionally important temples are built in the native style, conscientiously and with fine results in the case of the great Higashi Hongwanji temples in Kyoto, but usually of the bastard Shinto that marks the Tokyo Shokonsha already referred to.

So far as one can see, the period of good architecture is over in Japan. The native attack on Buddhism two centuries ago was the beginning of the end; the restoration of Shinto was its continuation, and the acceptance of Western civilization was its consummation. For thirteen centuries it has developed as civilization progressed, each period perfecting some special quality, until it reached its climax of splendour under the first of the Tokugawa Shogun. It is now a dead style, a thing of the past, and with all other manifestations of art in Japan must forever remain so un-

[1] Since superseded by Frank Lloyd Wright's exceedingly "modernist" and emancipated structure, which escaped destruction in the earthquake and fire.

less some not impossible revolution brings back the great ideals and wholesome principles of the past.

We have now considered the historical development of Japanese architecture from its beginning in the sixth century to its apparent extinction in the last years of the nineteenth century. Examined so it is seen to follow the lines of all other architectural history, expressing very accurately the changing conditions of civilization. Like other architectural styles it is a consistent, logical development from the conditions that brought it into existence, and it demands and should receive the same respect and study that are devoted to the styles of the West. It is true that, so aloof is it from Western ideals and methods of thought, it can never serve so completely as a model for contemporary work as those styles of Europe with which we in America have such close kinship and sympathy.

On the other hand, it is possible for us to learn many most valuable lessons from it. In the first place we shall see how delicately buildings of all kinds may be made to fit themselves to their surroundings. In this respect the architecture of Japan acknowledges no superior. Nothing could be more subtle and sympathetic than the relationship between the temples and pagodas, the castles, cottages, and inns, and their natural surroundings. In every line and mass the harmony is complete. The buildings seem almost to be a concentration and perfection of the hills and trees of which they seem to be a part. One feels this particularly when looking on any structure designed on Western lines, no matter how excellent it may be according to European standards. The native work is a part of the country, the foreign is ugly, ungrammatical, offensive.

Another quality that is most salient is the exceeding unity and perfection of composition either of single temples or of whole groups, either of the exterior or the interior. The whole thing is built up with the utmost subtlety of feeling and delicacy of appreciation until it forms a consistent and united whole. The refinements of line and proportion have their equals only in the architecture of Greece and medieval Europe. The mere measuring of some one of the older buildings reveals a subtlety of feeling for proportion that is amazing. Such measurements show at once that every curve and every line has been developed with the most astonishing care.

Still another quality that could be studied to advantage is that of the extreme solemnity of the temple interiors. For impressiveness and deeply religious feeling, together with extreme splendour of colouring and wealth of detail, they are almost unexcelled. The Gothic interiors of Europe have their own quality of awe-inspiring majesty which no other architecture has ever approached, but for effects of dusky splendour Byzantine and Japanese architecture stand together.

It is when we come to the domestic work of Japan, however, that we find more in the way of salutary teaching. Of course the Japanese private house in plan and construction is utterly foreign to Western conditions and requirements. Indeed, were it not for the amazing hardiness and indifference to cold which characterize the people, it would hardly do even for Japan, for it is probably a development from Southern types. For a tropical climate it is beyond criticism, but in the cold winters of northern Japan, it leaves much to be desired. It has certain qualities, however, that we could imitate to advantage. One of these is the perfect simplicity of each room, with its soft mats, its beautiful wood, its subtle colouring, its reserved and satisfying decorations. A Japanese room is full of repose, and after one has come to feel these qualities fully, one remembers with a kind of horror the stuffy chaos of the apartments in a modern American dwelling.

Perhaps the greatest lesson one learns in Japan is that of the beauty of natural wood, and the right method of treating it. The universal custom of the West has been to look on wood as a convenient medium for the obtaining of ornamental

forms through carving and joinery, the quality of
the material itself being seldom considered. In
Japan the reverse is the case. In domestic work a
Japanese builder shrinks from anything that
would draw attention from the beauty of his
varied woods. He treats them as we do precious
marbles, and one is forced to confess that under
his hand wood is found to be quite as wonderful
a material as our expensive and hardly worked
marble. In Japan one comes to the final conclusion that stains, paint, and varnish, so far as interior work is concerned, are nothing short of artistic crimes.

In another respect Japanese builders are right
and we are wrong. They do not destroy that
sense of protection every room should possess,
by filling whole sides thereof with plate glass.
Instead their windows are of delicate lattice work
covered with translucent paper, and the result is
a light that is soft and pleasant. Nothing can be
more absurd than our modern fashion of filling
an entire window opening with one or two sheets

of glass, particularly when, as happens in cities, there is no possible reason for looking out of doors.

There are many minor lessons of similar nature which we would do well to learn from the East, and these lessons it is perfectly possible to take to heart and adapt, without copying the qualities which are expressive of a civilization radically different to ours. Such copying would be affectation, but the profiting by the lessons set before us would be simple common sense.

TEMPLES AND SHRINES

THERE is a certain curious attitude of mind, a legacy from the old days when the mental ports of the West were as inexorably barred as were the territorial ports of the East, that still continues with misdirected fidelity to look on Buddhism as simply one of the many forms of horrid idolatry lightly to be overthrown by missionary zeal, and on its architectural monuments, the ancient temples that still stand between the western waters of India and the farthest land of Japan, as on the foolish haltings of poor savages, ethnically interesting, perhaps, but most improper, and reprehensible to all right-minded Christian students.

There is another that abases itself before kakemono, cloisonné and jade, netsuke and porcelain, wood-carvings, embroideries, and lacquer, finding them all a revelation of art, but that ignores the architecture and sculpture of the land of its artistic idolatry, holding it strange, and therefore impossible.

As a religion and a philosophy, Buddhism brought into existence the brilliant civilization that expressed itself in the vigorous and fanciful character, the noble feudalism, and the exquisite art of Japan, but as the cathedrals of medieval Europe stand closer to their inspiring cause than the industrial art of the time, so do the temples of Japan express more clearly and truly the power that brought them into being, than do the kakimono and netsuke that have monopolized the admiration of students.

If the time is ever to come when Japan is to accept the Catholic Christianity of the West, then its apostles must understand that which they are to supplant, not scorn it; they must meet a pagan but lofty civilization on its own ground, and offer their gift, not as to a barbarian tribe of African fetish worshipers, but as the Apostles offered it to the Athenians, respecting what they had come to destroy. For Japan is by nature a deeply religious nation; she is possessed of two highly developed systems, dwelling side by side in perfect harmony — Shinto and Buddhism; one of incalculable age, with a thorough system of Christian ethics, and laws of duty and obedience that are almost without rival in the world and that have justified themselves by that marvelous product, Japanese chivalry; one, also vastly old, though dating here from but fourteen centuries ago, a mystic and delicate religious system, a philosophy so profound and at the same time so scientific that it has always commanded the deep respect of all Western scholars. Together these religions have built up one of the most wonderful of nations, developed a character of exceeding nobility, brought into existence a noble culture and a high artistic spirit, created and maintained a potent and penetrating civilization.

Thousands of temples and monasteries, tens of

thousands of priests and religious of both sexes, millions of adherents of every social class, a vigour of devotion that has just created the largest and most costly Buddhist temple in Japan, little shrines in every household, public worship, prayers and pilgrimages are the outward manifestations of a faith the West is striving to supersede. Such an undertaking calls for the very flower of Christian civilization to match the descendants of long lines of knights and nobles, many of whom have obtained degrees at Oxford and Cambridge.

Such a priest I had the privilege of knowing in Kyoto at the great temple of Nishi Hongwanji, founded in the mid-thirteenth century by Kenshin Daishi. He was a graduate of Oxford, a master of many languages, a careful student of Herbert Spencer, a scholar of the utmost erudition, of noble and knightly blood, a living exposition of high breeding and courtly manners; withal a poet, a philosopher, and a connoisseur.

As I sat before this calm and courtly ecclesiastic, a model of so nearly all that is admirable in men, surrounded by the masterpieces of the great painters of the seventeenth century, it was impossible to refrain from drawing a contrast between certain of the denominational missionaries I had met and this grave representative of an august philosophy, with his slow smile and his unfathomable eyes, and to wonder how long it would take the man of the West to convert him of the East, and to gather into his own particular fold the sheep now beneath the care of the priest of Nishi Hongwanji.

To understand the essential qualities either of Buddhism or " The Way of the Gods " is for the Western mind almost an impossibility; one may read and reread the Sutras and the Kojiki and strive to fathom the meaning of the commentators thereon; there is a final secret, the soul of Buddhism, that has never been written in words, for it cannot be expressed so to the intelligence, and there is a certain quality in Shinto that finds no voicing in its visible shape. But it is at least possible for us to become familiar with the outward forms of this faith, the temples, the sacred art, the liturgies and the ritual, and through these to appreciate in a measure the fact that the power that brought them into being was no wile of Satan, but indeed a partial manifestation of the God " Who has never left Himself without a witness."

Japan is the offspring of two religions, Shinto and Buddhism: the first, one of those forms of tribal or ethnic religions compounded of nature and ancestor worship; the second a most exalted form of spiritual philosophy, one of the most profound that man has ever achieved. Under the sole dominion of the first, the inhabitants of the Japanese archipelago had made no very startling advance, but they had been prepared for the coming of the vitalizing fire of Buddhism, the ground had been made ready, the seed only was wanting. In the year 552 the first wave of the great Buddhist tide of missionary activity touched the shores of Yamato in the shape of cer-

tain Korean priests sent by the King of Pakché.
Forty years later Prince Shotoku Taishi, regent
of the Empire under the Empress Suiko, accepted
the new faith, and from that moment civilization
began. The great monastery of Horiuji was the
first Buddhist foundation, and it was completed
substantially in its present shape in 607. Al-
though built wholly of wood, three of the original
buildings are still standing, the great gate,
Azeku-no-mon, the main temple or Kondo, and
the pagoda or Go-ju-to. The other buildings,
though restorations, are accurate reproductions
of those destroyed through process of time.

Architecturally all are pure Sino-Korean of
the sixth century, one of the most extraordinary
architectural styles in the world, for it is the
counterpart of the Romanesque of the south of
France, and the two styles bear exactly the same
relation to the root style of Greece, with the single
exception that in the West there was no change
in materials, while in the East there was a reversion to the original and primitive wood. From

Athens to Asia Minor, thence to Persia and so to India, architecture, painting and sculpture worked their way back against the sun and over provinces where still remained traces of enormously ancient civilization. Bit by bit the original impulse was modified and took on new forms: the mysterious and mystical East entered in, dominated and revolutionized the Hellenic impulse, and at last, when the great progression reached China, the genius of old Cathay brought the final change. Mysticism and meditation, the soul of the infinite East, had wrought out of alien shards its own intimate and exquisite habiliments. In the West action and conduct and the spirit of innovation, driven by dominant Christianity, had transmuted the original Greek through the decadent Roman, into the vigorous, aggressive, practical Romanesque; in the East mysticism and tradition, guided by the subtleties of Buddhism, had wrought their own intimate change.

When at last the limit of land was reached and

the advance guard of the new life of the East stood on the shores of the confining sea, almost the last vestige of Hellenic forms was gone, and only in the entasis of the columns of the great gate and in the thin folds and studied calmness of the sculptured drapery of the statues are to be seen the lurking traces of Greek art, and within a few years these also were to disappear, giving free field for the full exercise of the indigenous Japanese spirit.

These few little temples on the outskirts of Nara are the most precious architectural monuments of Japan: together with the marvelous statues of their own and the succeeding century, they are priceless documents in the history of the art of the world. From the seventh to the twelfth centuries, China and Japan stood as the most highly civilized countries of the globe, the Eastern Empire and the Khalifates of Spain their only rivals, and therefore their art was the most perfect then existing. With the development of monasticism and feudalism in Europe, Christian civilization took the lead, but for six centuries the East bore the banner of art and civilization.

It is in this light that we must consider the art of Japan, her sculpture, painting, industrial art, and particularly her religious architecture, as the visible expression of the highest civilization then existing in the world, a civilization that was brave, loyal, upright, lofty in its ideals, based on a religion and a philosophy that were in their esoteric aspect " mystic, wonderful," while exoterically they were simple, intimate, and comforting. From the standpoint of the casual traveler, even of the architect, Japanese architecture is at first absolutely baffling; it is like Japanese music, so utterly foreign, so radically different in its genesis, so aloof in its moods and motives from the standards of the West, that for a long time it is a wonder merely, a curiosity, a toy perhaps or a sport of nature, not a serious product of the human mind, a priceless contribution to the history of the world. Partly by inheritance, partly by education, we have been qualified for thinking in one way, and in one way only. From Athens through Rome, Byzantium, the Auvergne, Normandy, the Ile de France, to Yorkshire and Somerset, there is running an easily traceable thread of unbroken continuity of architectural tradition, but from Athens through Ionia, Persia, Hindustan, China, and Korea, to Japan, while the line is equally continuous, it is through lands aloof and barred, and by ways that are blind and bewildering. We can think forward in the terms of the West, we can hardly think backwards in the terms of the mysterious East.

Yet when the revolution is accomplished and the rebellious mind is bent to the unfamiliar course, this strange architecture comes to show itself in its true light. It is more nearly Greek than any other, for it is the perfecting of a single, simple, and primitive mass by almost infinite refinements of line and proportion. The Gothic cathedrals and abbeys of Europe were monuments of mighty genius, unconsciously created under the influence of overmastering emotion:

the temples of Horiuji, Nara, Uji, and Kyoto were the result of a conscious and Hellenic striving for the ultimate perfection in line and curve and form. Note in the pictures of Horiuji, Uji, Nara, the sinuous following of line, the steely curves of the roofs, the massing of the shadows, the fretting of the light and shade — they are all the final things; beyond them is no further possibility. There is nothing in the Parthenon more keenly perfect than the sweep of the roof angles; nothing in the Erechtheion more graceful and mobile than the Imperial pavilion of the Fujiwara, now the Ho-o-do of Byodo-in.

But there is a greater quality in these early temples than these that are purely architectural; they are full of a spiritual import that is quite overpowering. They breathe mysticism and abstraction, they are dreamlike and visionary. Under their shadows alone could one understand a little of Buddhism. In the vast lines of their sweeping roofs, in the ordered symmetry of their sword-like curves, in the majesty of their lines, the solemn harmony of their composition, there is so much of the dim and occult East that they seize upon the imagination like some subtle enchantment. It is not until we come to the later temples, those of the Fujiwara, Ashikaga, and Tokugawa Shogunates that we find the wonderful interiors, dim and silent, sweet with incense and splendid with the glory of cinnabar lacquer and beaten gold. These early temples are homely and barren within, gray plaster spotted with ancient Indian frescoes fading softly away, and round columns of bare, unpolished wood. A jealous government has removed the greatest of the statues, and only a few are left to tell the tale of primal glory.

The effect comes from the exterior alone; and here if we can once disabuse our minds of the preconceptions of the West, it is powerful and direct. Proportion, composition, and the following of line, these are the three architectural triumphs of the Sino-Korean architecture of Buddhism, and they are so victorious, so ultimate, that we can only admit that the power that brought them into being was a power of beneficence and might.

When Buddhism came to Japan, bringing a highly developed style of architecture, it found the racial religion housing itself in huts barbarous in their nature and differing but slightly from the rough dwellings of the people; walls of posts and planks formed the enclosure, and this was roofed with sloping poles forming a steep gable and projecting through the heavy thatch in X form. The ridge was kept in place by transverse logs of unhewn timber, and this was, so far as we know, absolutely all. The temples of Ise, the most holy of the Shinto shrines, are supposed to be exact copies of originals built long before the Christian era, but as the Shinto law is that these same temples must be razed and reconstructed every twenty years, it is quite possible that modifications may have occurred. In any case they are sufficiently ugly and barbarous.

The splendid architecture of China superseded

all this with scant delay, and scarcely an hundred years after the building of the Horiuji temples, the Japanese, emancipated from barbarism, began the work of developing the Chinese style on their own lines. The pagoda of Yakushiji is, I think, the oldest existing building in which one finds the native spirit working itself out, and it is a very wonderful building indeed, brilliant in its conception, radical in its originality, yet faithful in its delicate proportions and its masterly composition to the classical type brought from the continent.

From this Yakushiji pagoda the progress was direct and unbroken through the epochs of Nara, Kyoto, Kamakura, and Yedo, until it culminated and ceased in the overwrought shrines of Shiba and Nikko and Uyeno; but simultaneously and amicably a more or less independent style was developing in the shape of the architecture of Shinto. For the new religion and the old were seldom intolerant of each other. Buddhism very wisely met the ethnic religion in friendliness,

cast over it something of the glory of its philosophy and the sweetness of its faith, and left it to
follow its course, which it forthwith proceeded
to do, treading obediently in the steps of the
greater power that represented the spiritual
achievements of all Asia. Little by little the rude
contrivance of Ise became transformed into the
comparative elaboration of Izumo, and for centuries Shinto architecture differed little from that
of Buddhism beyond the fact that it sternly re-
jected colour, that it was always parsimonious
in its giving of carving and other decoration, that
it refused roof tiles and held by the traditional
thick thatch of velvety hinoki bark, and that it
retained the semblance of the X rafters and the
transverse logs of the ridge (Plate XVII). Shinto
added nothing either to the architecture of Buddhism, or that of the world, for the triumphant
torii, one of the most perfectly simple, exquisite,
and classical forms ever evolved in the art of
building, is the creation of Ryobu-shinto, in other
words, of Buddhism. The primitive torii was

XVII A Contemporary Shinto Shrine

XVIII A Torii

simply two vertical posts connected at the top by a cross beam, all of unhewn wood: it possessed no element of beauty whatever. Buddhism, profoundly, monumently wise, recognizing the indestructible power of immemorial tradition, made no attempt to sweep away the primitive cult, but accepted it, metamorphosed it, cast around it the glory of its own supreme spirituality — and won the whole nation. The torii (Plate XVIII), no longer a perch for sacrificial fowl, ugly and barbarous in its details, became the symbol of all that is sacred, and in its exquisite proportions and subtle lines it is wholly worthy of its new function.

I may be wrong, but it seems to me that there is a lesson here for us. We send our worthy missionaries to Japan, and so far as those of the Protestant denominations are concerned, they only too often begin by condemning as entirely damnable every truth as well as every pious practise of Shinto and Buddhism. This means absolute failure, and for just so long as this course is pursued. The whole civilization of Japan, and the fundamental character of its people, are the product of Shinto and of Buddhism. No group of missionaries can destroy these in ten thousand years. Now a good half of Shinto, and even more of Buddhism, are wholesome, helpful, and true: still more is capable of modification to bring it into harmony with Christianity. Let us accept these things, win confidence by our charity, and little by little bring the desired reforms to pass. Let us take the rude " bird rest " and change it into the glorified torii. In twenty years Japan would be a Christian nation, still possessing the splendid qualities of her national character that we should try to supplement, not to supplant.

It is a great artistic catastrophe that an inordinate passion for fighting on the part of the strenuous Japanese, coupled with the perishable nature of their building materials, should have resulted in the almost total destruction of the religious architecture that came into existence between the last years of the seventh century and

the first year of the seventeenth. From the great
Fujiwara or Kyoto period, extending from
A.D.700 to the triumph of Yoritomo in 1192,
nothing whatever remains except the marvelous
Ho-o-do of Byodo-in at Uji. This exquisite
" Phœnix Hall," originally a pleasure pavilion
of the splendid Shogun, is now a temple; and as
one first sees it in the dusk of early evening perhaps, rising above the dark little tarn clogged
with pale iris, it seems like a dream or some magical fancy of Kublai Khan. It is a figment of the
imagination, not a solid fabric in time and space.
Viewed architecturally it reaches the highest
level in point of composition and design. Sober-
ness and restraint form its solid foundation, the
subtlest feeling for curve-composition vitalizes it
into being, and delicate fancy glorifies it as a
garment. Once the central hall was one wealth of
incrustation, ebony, ivory, silver, mother of
pearl: now it is crumbling and desolate, traces
only of decoration clinging to the walls and
fretted ceiling. What Japan must have been in

the thousand years of the great Fujiwara dynasty we can only conjecture from this one priceless building, rising like the ghost of an empire
from the tea fields of Uji.

In Kyoto itself three temples only still stand
as records of the next two Shogunates — the
San-ju-san-gen-do, built in 1266 and restored in
1662, an inferior and valueless structure at best,
and the Ginkaku-ji and Kinkaku-ji, the last two
pleasure pavilions of the Ashikaga Shoguns.
Graceful and pleasing as they are, they are too
playful, too essentially domestic in their style, to
serve as any indication of the temple architecture
of the time. Such temples as there are that date
from this period, chiefly those of Kamakura and
its environs, have been too completely restored
and rebuilt to serve any useful purpose, and we
must come down another century to the year
1603, when Iyeyasu founded the Tokugawa Shogunate and transferred his capital to Yedo.

From the two centuries following this date
come practically all the existing temples, and

XIX Type of Revised Enryaku

XX Kasuga Gate, Nara

they are legion: in style they are very varied, from classical simplicity to a degree of gorgeous elaboration that is almost inconceivable; from an affected reversion to Chinese and Korean types to a daring originality that is without precedent. In one town we shall find a vast and imposing structure barren of colour, sparingly touched with carving; in another a little shrine riotous in sculptured wood and covered, every inch of it, with blazing colour and lacquer of gold and ebony and cinnabar. For three-fourths of this epoch of two centuries the old laws of proportion and composition held in force, and during this time the Tokugawa temples were almost worthy of equal honour with those of the seventh and thirteenth centuries.

Broadly speaking, they fall into three stylistic classes, Enryaku, Ashikaga, and Tokugawa proper. The Enryaku style (Plate XIX) is one based with more or less accuracy on the traditions and drawings of the temples built at the beginning of the Kyoto era by the Mikado

Kwammu. This is that style developed by the Japanese themselves from the Chinese norm introduced two centuries earlier. The buildings are low and comparatively simple; there is no carving or painted decoration, and the colour is the simplest; pure white plaster and wood painted with red oxide of lead. This was the favourite style of the temples of the Ryobu-Shinto sect, a friendly and philosophical amalgamation of Shinto and Buddhist theology, swept away about a century ago by a curious and fantastic movement toward the restoration of " pure Shinto." Many of the shrines and temples still stand, however, though shorn of the richness of accessories and ritual borrowed from Buddhism. The Kasuga temples of Nara are fine examples of this style; and as their flaming white and red flashes out in the midst of the enormous cedar trees, hung with festoons of purple wistaria, they are certainly picturesque and even beautiful. (Plate XX.)

The Ashikaga temples are those that in their

largeness of parts, their grandeur of proportion, and their reliance on carving for their decoration, hark back to the reserved work of the fourteenth and fifteenth centuries. This is the favourite style of the Shin, the greatest of all the Buddhist sects and dating from the year 1224. The Higashi Hongwanji in Nagoya, and the great new temple of the same sect in Kyoto, serve to show the grandeur, even the sublimity, of these mighty structures. The great gates in this particular style are perhaps the most noble of all the different buildings. It really seems as though the perfection of composition, the subtle relation of parts and rhythm of line, had been achieved in these monumental gates.

More than any other of the Japanese architectural styles this development of the Ashikaga model seems to be the perfect translation into visible form of the spirit of Japanese feudalism and the equally perfect development of structural form from the qualities of the natural environment. The connection between these brown and gray temples and the forests and fields, rocks and rivers and mountains, is intimate and exact: as the castles and abbeys of England blend with her landscape and her air, as the nacreous palaces and shrines of Venice grow out of the opal sea, as the hot sandstone fortresses of Hindustan rear their blistered walls from the desert sands, or the marble miracles of tomb and pleasure house flash above still pools and in the midst of tropical gardens, so, and with equal intimacy, do these brown and weathered temples rest in the purple shadow of gnarled cryptomeria or lift themselves from the shoulders of deep-wooded hills. With infinite craft, priests and artists and gardeners have wrought a perfect setting for their shrines, piling long flights of stone steps up the broken hillsides, raising ramparts and terraces, training the willing trees into strange architectural forms, blending the whole as a painter blends his colours, composing the lines and masses as he builds his pictorial masterpiece.

With the third and most sumptuous develop-

ment of architecture, or rather decoration, the
true Tokugawa style, the last development from
the distant Sino-Korean norm, far back in the
beginnings of things, a thousand years ago, culminated and crumbled away. Japanese civilization had always expressed itself in some chosen
form of art: first of all in sculpture; then, a little
later, during the last half of the Fujiwara Shogunate, in literature; then in architecture, under
the Hojo and early Ashikaga; then in painting
for the last half of the latter dynasty; and finally,
in decoration combined with painting, for the
first half of the Tokugawa régime. For two and
a half centuries, from 1400 to 1650, from Cho-
Densu to Korin, Japanese painting had followed
a course of almost unexampled glory. Sesshu,
Josetu, Shubun, the immortal Kano Motonubu
and the four other masters of the same wonderful house, together with scores of lesser men, had
raised Japan to the very highest plane among
artistic nations. Unkei and Hidari Jingoro had
made of wood-carving a fine-art, not unworthy

to stand with the contemporary painting. Together, these two arts were in the constant service of architecture and there came a complete
and radical change in religious building: from the
palaces of the Mikado and the nobles the splendid screens and wall paintings, kakemono and
ramma, crept into the monasteries and so into
the temples themselves. Gold leaf and burnished
lacquer took the place of natural wood and dull
colour decoration: carved cinnabar lacquer and
elaborate metal work engulfed the altars and
shrines, and Japanese architecture burst from its
brown chrysalis a flaunting butterfly painted
with the hues of dreams.

Apart from Hagia Sophia, St. Mark's in Venice and the Cappella Palatina in Palermo, I
know of no religious interiors that can vie with
such caves of glory as Chion-in. (Plate XXI.)
Words simply fail when an attempt is made
to describe the unparalleled splendour of such
temples. Black lacquer and gold and cinnabar;
chiseled baldachinos of exquisite metal work;

XXI Interior of Shari-den, Horiuji

XXII A Buddhist High-Altar

massive ropes and tassels of blood-red silk; censers of gold and silver and bronze; great lotus plants sheeted with beaten gold; vestments of stiff brocade heavy with massed embroidery; deep-tongued bells, sonorous drums; strange, unearthly chanting of tonsured bonzes; clouds of pale incense — it is all like some vision out of the mysterious, intangible past, aloof, unapproachable.

And nowhere, not for one minute fraction of an inch, is there any failure of faultless art. In St. Mark's are tawdry anilin paper flowers against the pala d'oro. Our Lady of Chartres is decked out in cheap finery of the theatrical costumer. St. Albans cathedral is desecrated by the Brummagem " Gothic " of the modern Vandal, the late Lord Grimthorpe; but here in Japan, where, with corrugated iron chapels and trade altar ornaments we are doing what we can in a religious way to paralyze the art instinct of the last artistic people in the world, the temples themselves still remain virgin and undefiled. If a man wants to see what good art can mean and be when it is unspotted by modernism, he must go, not to Italy, or France or England, but to the Buddhist temples of Japan. (See Plate XXII.)

When Iyeyasu, the founder and first Shogun of the Tokugawa dynasty, died, his son Iyemitsu began the erection of the tombs and shrines of Nikko (Plate XXIII), the last word of religious architecture in Japan. With the temples of Shiba and Uyeno and Tokyo they form an episode in themselves, unhealthy, exotic, decadent. That they are in a way supremely beautiful is perfectly true — they are the apotheosis of coloured and carved decoration; but it is beauty gone mad, and bursting beyond all bounds. It was precisely what was happening in the West, luxury sucking the heart out of art, the fire of genius burning itself away in the enormous pageant of a palpitating aurora. The glory was unspeakable, but the ashes that remained were dry and dead. The fire had burned itself out.

Then came the opening of the ports, the revolution, the restoration of the Mikado, the abolition of feudalism, the disestablishment of Buddhism, the rehabilitation of the Shinto anomaly, and the Constitution. Feudal and Buddhist civilization crumbled, and nothing permanent seemed to take its place. Occidentalism became a Black Death to the arts of Japan, and for a time the outlook was dreary indeed. Latterly, however, things are brightening a little. Buddhism is pulling itself together and becoming aggressive. Shinto in its religious aspect is becoming little more than an edict. There is a healthy rebellion against Western canons of painting, and a few strong men are carefully gathering up the scattered shards of the past, nourishing the flickering fires of art that had not wholly died away. There is a strong revulsion of feeling toward the good artistic models of a few centuries ago. From this will result one of two things, either an archæological Frankenstein, soulless, dead, doomed to sudden extinction, or a knitting up of the raveled cord of history; a new lease of life for artistic Japan, a new era of esthetic glory. At present it is impossible to say what will be the issue.

XXIII Before the Shrine of Iyeyasu

XXIV At Shiogama

TEMPLE GARDENS

In the dim gardens of mouldering Buddhist monasteries one may still find, as in the temples themselves, hints of the old Japan. The sacred tradition that has preserved the original forms of eighth century architecture through a long sequence of structures built only to be consumed and again restored, has held as well in the surrounding gardens, and though nothing may remain of the ancient originals, save only the fantastic stones (far-sought and eagerly treasured), the curves of the walks are still the same, the placing of the shrubs and flowers and gnarled, dwarf trees unchanged, and even the patterns traced in the silver sand are the patterns of long ago.

They are very fascinating, these temple gardens, and they have a character wonderful in its

diversity. Sometimes they are nothing more than
the necessary fore-courts of minor temples: a
terrace, a few steps, a lantern or two (Plate
XXV), a grinning stone dog or benignant image
of Jizo " The Helper," and perhaps a crabbed
tree or bush of scented box. Then they become
solemn and ghostly graveyards crowded with
ranks of gray and moss-covered monuments of
strangely beautiful shapes, leaning, all of them,
from the jostling of endless earthquakes; the
newer ones — yes, and some of those hoary with
antiquity — blurred by the thin smoke of burning incense sticks and fronted by sections of bamboo holding freshly cut flowers. Again they
blossom into the full glory of the stately and
hieratic garden, the domain of nature glorified by
consummate art, where rocks and sand and
water, lotus, iris, peony, azalea and the royal
fuji, box and maple, pine and cherry, are all
blended into one wonderful setting for the scarlet
temple that flames in the midst against its back-
ground of forest or serrated hill.

XXV In the Forest of Nara

XXVI GARDEN OF SHOREN-IN, KYOTO

Yet, whatever its estate, the temple garden is less a *pleasaunce* than a framework; it is like every good garden, a modulation from pure nature to pure art. In the old temple of Horenji at Shiogama (Plate XXIV), you may see how finely everything leads up to the lofty temple, and the effect must have been finer yet when the shrine was still Buddhist and before the Shinto priests who now control it raised the rather clumsy torii at the foot of the dizzy flight of steps. Again at Nara, rocks, box, lotus, palm and pine are all placed just where they will do most honour to the temple itself, and together with this compose into the picture that is perfect and complete.

A picture always, you must note: line, texture, form and colour, all are duly and delicately considered, and a space of garden is composed with all the laborious study that goes to the making of a screen or kakemono. How perfectly the whole thing composes at Shoren-in (Plate XXVI), the curve of the bridge, the sharp angle of the steps, the convolutions of volcanic rock, the clean cleavages of the slate chased with exquisite ideography; and in colour, silver gray slate stones and lichened granite, green bronze, and the deeper green of cryptomeria leaves. Or again in the shrines of Uyeno consider how wisely the garden itself is reduced to the simplest forms, gravel and flat stones and a few big bronze lanterns. Here the cherry trees are supreme and they are given full sway; flowers and shrubs are banished for they are unnecessary. The great trees do their full work; yet this is good gardening, and quite as legitimate as would be the case were all the flowers of the earth brought under requisition.

A Japanese gardener can work with anything — or almost nothing.

There is a legend of a royal garden, built long ago by a man who gave to the task ten years of his life and half the wealth of a great daimyo, a garden that appealed to every varying emotion of the soul, and worked its will like a great symphony, where only one of the products of the earth was employed, and that was simply and only — rocks. Even now these are sought carefully from every province, and some curious or beautiful specimen is hoarded like a jewel. How valuable, indeed how quite indispensable these may be, can be seen, though imperfectly, from almost any of the illustrations, particularly from those of Ishi-yama-dera. (Plate XXVII.) The name of this ancient temple on Lake Biwa means simply, "The Temple of the Rocky Mountain," for there is a curious outcropping here of black and contorted basalt, and every crag has been used as part of a scheme of gardening.

It would be hard to imagine anything more delicate and crafty than the manner in which the monks have built up their picture. Every native quality of the rock is emphasized and its effect enhanced by a clever and ingenious art. The smooth foreground of shining sand, the fluffy green of the forest, the soft verdure of delicate

shrubs sprouting from rocky crevices, the smooth velvet of hinoki thatch and weathered wood, the clean angles of chiseled stone, all these things are handled like the colours of a painter's palette, they are placed with discretion, fused and blended, and finally composed into perfectly united wholes.

Almost every temple garden has a peculiar quality, some one feature that is dominant and sets the keynote, as it were. Here at Ishiyama it is volcanic rock, in Uyeno it is the cherry, at Kamakura the lotus, at Nara the purple fuji, at Nikko druidic cryptomeria guard the shrines of the dead Shogun. At the Nishi Hongwanji in Kyoto, again, water seems almost to play the principal part, while at the gardens of the Ginka-kuji it is white sand wrought into mounds and delicate pavement patterns. Here is " The Platform of Silver Sand " and beyond it " The Mound that Looks Toward the Moon " consecrated by the lordly Yoshimasa and still heaped as for the great Shogun's enthronement, though

XXVII The Garden of Ishi-yama

four centuries and more have passed since he became one with the gods.

Whatever the keynote it holds throughout the composition, as at Shiogama the tall gray masts of the cryptomeria are echoed and emphasized by the vanishing lines of the enormous steps, the slim verticals of the white staffs, and the uprights of the granite torii.

And how wonderful a thing in itself is this same consummate form of the torii. It is the noblest and simplest gateway ever devised and it adds a crowning touch to many a temple garden, though it is the sign of religious and philosophical primitivism. When scores of these vermilion torii are grouped together over gray stone steps in the midst of bronze-green cryptomeria, the effect is one of splendid colour hardly to be matched elsewhere.

It is not around the great and famous temples that one finds the most alluring gardens, but in out-of-the-way spots, in forgotten valleys where foreign feet have seldom trod. Across the river from Uji I found one such garden in a hill temple I had never heard named before, Koshoji. There is a river road up to where the tumbling Ujigawa bursts through a cleft in the hills, and following this one suddenly comes upon a long straight path cut through dense black trees, rising steep from the river, and closed at the summit by a gleaming white Korean gateway. (Plate XXVIII.) As one approaches, nothing is visible but this same gate with its arched opening in the white plastered base, surmounted by the intricate bracketing of its curved roof, long, plastered walls reaching away on either hand, and above, the low sweeping roofs of gray-green tile, and, in April, as when I saw it, a great cloud of pink vapour poised over all, the amazing blossoming of an ancient cherry.

One comes out from under the white arch with a sudden catching of the breath. It is not a large temple, indeed it is hardly more than a toy, one of those still, little monasteries asleep in a forgotten eddy of the turbulent river of change; but

XXVIIIa Koshoji Gate, Uji

XXVIIIb A Monastery Garden, Kyoto

XXIXa THE FORE-COURT, KOSHOJI

XXIXb KOSHOJI GARDEN

it is the more charming for all that. The Nishi and Higashi Hongwanji temples of Kyoto, the almost terrifying monster belonging to the latter sect in Nagoya, the complex and amazingly elaborate Obaku-san just a little way down the river, these vast and ceremonious structures crush one with the very majesty of their noble architecture; but for charm and fascination and keen appeal, one must search out tiny sanctuaries like this of Koshoji.

One enters first a little fore-court surrounded by buildings on three sides, the fourth being filled by the wall and gateway. (Plate XXVIII.) The hondo or preaching hall is in front, a low simple building; on the left is the residence, on the right the library and the bell cage. All the buildings are raised on low stone-walled terraces: there are few flowers, and the gardening is made up almost wholly of box and white sand. Of course there is the great pink tree, but its glory lasts for a short ten days in the spring, and for the rest of the year the scented box is supreme.

Nothing could be finer than these great rounded masses of bronze green: they rise from the white sand like tropical islands from a phosphorescent sea, and their clean-cut contours come crisp and fine against the pearly plaster of the convent walls.

In this fore-court all is trim and formal, but if you pass through a little gate in the farther left-hand corner, you come upon a very different scene. (Plate **XXIX.**) Here everything is wildly picturesque, though still on a tiny scale; the monastic buildings wander off at all angles until they are brought up standing against the wall of a beetling hill from which the trees lean down, thrusting their twisted branches out over the tiled roofs with their long, keen curves. From under the very temple, it seems, springs a minute mountain torrent threading its way through the midst of the garden at the bottom of a Lilliputian crevasse. Toy stone bridges are flung across it, little trees twisted into most impossible curves and angles jut from its banks, velvety box runs

along the mossy stone embankment, and strange
little wild flowers seek the edge of the water.
There are bronze lanterns and vases also, and
on the farther side the moss-blackened grave-
stones begin and lead one away over the flat step-
ping stones to the hill base, then up the slope
where the whole forest is full of similar memo-
rials of the dead.

This Koshoji is full of some kind of enchantment, once there one would never leave. We had
heard each evening down at our inn at Uji (our
inn that was built far back in the days of Hideyoshi) the velvety boom of some enormous bell,
a sound that seemed to draw one irresistibly to
rise up in the still night and search for its source
under the great, pale moon. In Koshoji we found
the bell, and much more; a little oasis in the desert of steam trams and beer and liberal politics,
and we wanted to stay there forever. The old
Japan has this charm, and I think it concentrates
itself and becomes really quite irresistible, in the
form of a scented temple garden in some forgot-

ten monastery, where the odour of incense min-
gles with that of box, where the patterned sand
retains the lines of a thousand years ago, where
tonsured bonzes in yellow robes move silently
through the shed petals of a pink cherry, and a
thunderous bell gives tongue at the rising of the
moon.

DOMESTIC INTERIORS

WHILE in public architecture, in painting and sculpture, in the industrial arts, and even in the greater part of the domestic architecture of the better class, Japan is fast losing all national quality, the houses of the lower and middle classes still preserve the beautiful characteristics of the old art, so unique, so refined, so wholly ethnic and national.

The nobles are making themselves uncomfortable and absurd in preposterous structures designed by third-rate English and German architects, and the same agency is responsible for shocking public buildings, vast in size, fearful and humiliating in design. Each year exhibitions are held in Uyeno Park where the pitiful attempts of Orientals to copy European modes of painting are held up to the awestruck admira-

tion of those that short-sightedly desire the death
of Japanese civilization, and to the pity and dis-
may of such Westerners as feel the glory of the
abandoned art and the futility and folly of the
movement that aims to establish in its place a
false theory, an alien ideal.

Yet there are wise and philosophical men in
Japan who fight strenuously against the foolish
fashion of Westernism, and are made to suffer
for it. Then there are architects who steadily refuse to have anything to do with foreign architecture in any of its forms. Such an one is my old
friend, Kashiwagi San, whose house is a faultless
model of native architecture, and who now and
then builds some delicate and exquisite house for
such of the nobility as are still unreconciled to the
new era in Japan. Thanks to these men and their
colleagues, and thanks also to the strong con-
servatism of the middle classes, Japanese domestic architecture is still a vital art, strong with a
life that may last even through the present inaus-
picious days, and form a basis for more logical

work, when the times have changed and national self-confidence is restored again.

The wonderful power and splendour of Japanese decorative art are a byword. The masterly sculpture of the seventh and eighth centuries is as yet rated only at a part of its value; native architecture is almost wholly unconsidered, or at least is dismissed as flimsy, erratic, undignified. I am sure this latter condemnation is wrong and that the national architecture is just as logical, just as firmly based on the enduring laws of art, as any other style in the world. It is the perfect style in wood, as Gothic may be called the perfect style in stone. Considered as an expression of profound and subtle artistic feeling through the mediumship of wood, it demands and must receive recognition and admiration. The great temples are the apotheosis of this system of building, but the private houses are its base, and in them one feels equally the logic of the construction, the clear knowledge of the essential beauty of the material.

To the Japanese, wood, like anything that possesses beauty, is almost sacred, and he handles it with a fineness of feeling that at best we only reveal when we are dealing with precious marbles. From all wood that may be seen close at hand, except such as is used as a basis for the rare and precious lacquer, paint, stain, varnish, anything that may obscure the beauty of texture and grain, is rigidly kept away. The original cost of the material is a matter of no consequence; if it has a subtle tone of colour, a delicate swirl in the veining, a peculiarly soft and velvety texture, it is carefully treasured and used in the place of honour.

The same respectful regard is shown towards plaster. With us of the West plaster is simply a cheap means of obtaining a flat surface that afterwards may be covered up in many different ways; with the Japanese plaster is an end in itself, and well it may be! We ourselves know nothing of the possibilities of this material. In Japan it has the solidity of stone, the colour of

XXX Wood, Plaster, Rice-paper, and Straw

smoke and mist and ethereal vapours, and the texture of velvet.

Wood and plaster: these are two of the four components of a Japanese interior. The third is woven straw of a pale, neutral green. This is for the inevitable mats that carpet all the floors. The fourth is rice paper; creamy white, thin and tough, stretched over the light latticework that forms the windows and the outer range of sliding screens (shoji), or covering the thicker screens (fusuma) that form the dividing partitions of the rooms. (Plate XXX.) Now and then these fusuma are covered with dull gold and faintly traced with dim landscapes or decorative drawings of birds and flowers, or else they are wrought with great black ideographs; sometimes the paper is faintly tinted, or varied by an admixture of delicate seaweed, but as a general thing, and except in a noble's " yashiki " or in some house of entertainment, the four materials remain: natural wood, tinted plaster, pleated straw, and rice paper.

Not an ambitious collection of materials, and yet for refinement, reserve, subtle colour, and perfection of artistic composition and ultimate effect, I know of few things to compare with the interior of a Japanese house.

For the extreme reserve that marks the architectural forms is echoed in the furnishings; they are few and of the utmost simplicity, nothing appearing except such articles as are absolutely necessary, and, inconsistent as it may appear with the common ideas of Japanese society, there is a certain austerity, asceticism even, about the native character that reduces this list of necessities much below what would be acceptable to Western ideas. A number of thin, flat, silk cushions to kneel on, one or two tansu, or chests of drawers, andon, or lamps with rice paper screens, small lacquered tables a foot square and half as high for serving food, hibachi or braziers, several folding screens, a standing mirror of burnished steel, and dishes of lacquer and porcelain form the entire list, with the exception of cooking utensils and the beds that are rolled up and put away in closets during the day. Under ordinary circumstances, a living-room, even of the best class, contains nothing in the way of furniture except what appears in the tokonoma and chigai-dana. Cushions are produced when the room is in use by day, beds at night, small tables when food is served, and a brazier if the weather is cold — this last apparently as a formality for it has no appreciable effect on the temperature. One would say that the result would be barren and cheerless, but this is not the case, every detail of form and colour being so exquisitely studied that the empty room is sufficient in itself. There is something about the great spacious apartments, airy and full of mellow light, that is curiously satisfying, and one feels the absence of furniture only with a sense of relief. Free from the rivalry of crowded furnishings, men and women take on a quite singular quality of dignity and importance. It is impossible after a time not to feel that the Japanese have adopted an idea of the function of a room and the method of best expressing this, far in advance of that which we have made our own.

From the moment one steps down from the kuruma and, slipping off one's shoes, passes into soft light and delicate colour, amongst the simple forms and wide spaces of a Japanese house there is nothing to break the spell of perfect simplicity and perfect artistic feeling; the chaos of Western houses becomes an ugly dream.

Except in the state residence or yashiki of daimyo (Plate XXXI) the entrance to a private house was usually without distinguishing marks, and one alighted at any portion of the narrow veranda or yen-gawa that surrounds the house, but in more pretentious structures the vestibule was a dominant feature and nowadays this emphasis has been borrowed from yashiki and temple and is found in all houses of the better sort. This vestibule is a square porch, open in front, with a wide, curved roof. At the end is a narrow wooden platform from which a big door gives ac-

XXXI A YASHIKI GATE

XXXII An Iri-kawa

XXXIII A MODERN ZASHIKI OR PARLOUR

XXXIV Tokonoma and Chigai-dana

cess to the grand corridor or iri-kawa that surrounds and isolates the state apartments. Opposite the door is a low, square, painted screen in a
lacquer frame, usually most gorgeously decorated; sometimes a dwarf tree stretches its
gnarled branches athwart the burnished gold, or
a great branch of blossoms in a precious vase
gives a note of splendid colour. The iri-kawa
(Plate XXXII) is a corridor from six to twelve
feet wide that serves at once as a passageway and
as a kind of anteroom to the chief apartment,
called jo-dan and ge-dan. When it leaves these
rooms of honour its name changes and it becomes
the ro-ka or passageway, giving access to the
parlours or zashiki (Plate XXXIII), the ante-
rooms or tamari, the tea-rooms or cha-dokoro.
In addition to these rooms are the kitchens,
baths, dressing-rooms, and servants' waiting-
rooms, but no bedrooms as such, for any apartment serves this latter purpose and also that of
a dining-room, the beds being made up on the
thick floor-mats, the meals brought by the

myriad servants to any part of the house and served on many little tables of red and black lacquer.

Nor does the arrangement or decoration of the rooms differ materially. Posts and beams of natural satiny wood, wonderful plaster of many subtle colours, ceilings of narrow timbers and delicately grained boards, floors covered with straw mats two inches thick and always three by six feet in size, this is the inevitable setting. In all the chief rooms one end is formed of two alcoves called tokonoma and chigai-dana (Plate XXXIV), the former to hold the picture or kakemono of the day, the other to display the selection of artistic treasures made from the stores ordinarily concealed in the fireproof kura or " godown." These two alcoves form the places of honour, and in feudal times the daimyo sat in front of them on the floor of the jo-dan, raised a step above the lower half of the room, or ge-dan where guests and retainers assembled to pay their respects. Now the guest is placed nearest the tokonoma while the host chooses a lower station.

In the chigai-dana and tokonoma are concentrated all the richness and decoration in the apartment. In the ancient palaces and yashiki they were of incredible magnificence, gold and lacquer, carving and precious woods forming a combination of almost unexampled richness (Plate XXXV); but in the modern house, while they remain very beautiful they have become comparatively simple and modest. In every case, however, they show to perfection the wonderful artistic feeling of the race, for in line and colour and form the combination of picture, flowers, and bric-à-brac is beyond criticism. One picture only is exposed in each room and this is changed daily. Is the master going a-fishing? Then some appropriate kakemono is hung in its place. Is it cherry time or the time of chrysanthemums or peonies or any other of the wonderful flowers of Japan? Then this feeling is echoed in the kakemono and in the flowers that stand in front. The whole basis of artistic combination may be gained in a study of Japanese tokonoma, for in them one finds preserved all the matchless refinement of feeling, all the result of centuries of artistic life that raised the art of Japan to the dizzy height from which Europe and America are now engaged in casting it ignominiously down.

In the ultimate analysis a Japanese house is seen to be simply a wide floor raised on posts two or three feet above the ground and matted with woven straw; covered by a low, tiled roof supported on many square posts and then divided into apartments by sliding screens of varying sizes. There are no windows as we know them and no doors.

Around the outside of the narrow veranda run the amado or storm screens of solid wood, closed tightly at night but pushed back into pockets during the day. On the inner side of this yengawa is the sliding wall of translucent rice paper screens, through which the light comes soft and mellow to the living rooms. Between the inner

XXXV A Stately Tokonoma

posts run the solid fusuma that may be removed
altogether, throwing the whole space into one
enormous apartment, should this be desired. In
modern times, permanent walls of plaster have
taken the place of some of the sliding screens, but
the greater part of the dividing partitions still
remain temporary and removable. Seldom more
than six and a half feet high, these fusuma have
a space between their tops and the ceiling and
this is filled with openwork panels or ramma,
often marvelously elaborate in design, their
delicate patterns coming black against the
pearly light that glows through the white
shoji.

Faultlessly cool, airy, and spacious in summer,
a Japanese house leaves much to be desired in
the cold winter of the north, for the wind filters
through every crack and crevice and the only
heat comes from charcoal braziers, beautiful in
design but wofully inadequate as heating agencies. But the Japanese are a strangely hardy race,
and clothed in thin silks sit comfortably in a tem-

perature that would chill an European to the marrow. Only in a bath is it possible for a foreigner to get warm, and here he is parboiled, for the temperature of the water ranges from 110° to 125°. A bath in a private house or hotel in Japan is, at first, something of an experience, for the bathroom is rather more public than any other apartment; in native inns indeed it is often open in front, giving, perhaps, on a court or garden, and it is possible for a guest to boil placidly in his tank and converse amicably with the other guests and the housemaids as they pass to and fro. But what it lacks in privacy the bath makes up in beauty, for it is often fantastic in design and elaborate in its decoration, with its walls of pierced woodwork, its lofty roof, and its floor of brilliant tiles.

In plan a private house is irregular and rambling to the last degree. The corridors reach off into long perspective, the rooms open out one after another, full of varying light and subtle colour; here and there little gardens appear in the most unexpected places, giving wonderful glimpses of pale bamboo groves and dwarfed trees and brilliant flowers, with silver sand underneath and tiny water courses paved with round pebbles. Great stone lanterns and bronze storks and dark pools of water are arranged with the most curious skill, and from every room one can look always either out to the great surrounding garden with its thick foliage and wandering brooks and curved bridges, or into the little enclosed courts, dim and damp and full of misty shadows.

The world offers few experiences more novel and charming than a visit to a Japanese house of the better class. The nation itself is hospitality incarnate, and to see this at its perfection one has only to possess himself of a letter of introduction to some conservative old noble. From the moment his kuruma stops under the great porch he is made to feel that the house is his, the host but an humble agent who has long waited the return of the rightful owner.

The 'ricksha rolls swiftly into the outer garden
and the brown-legged kurumaya gives a long,
wailing cry of warning. Hardly has the 'ricksha
stopped when the vestibule doors are slid back
and between them appears an old porter in blue-
gray silk, kneeling and bowing solemnly until his
head almost touches the floor. Shoes are slipped
off in the porch, and following the noiseless porter one is ushered into an anteroom to kneel on
silk cushions while his card is taken to the master. Presently the fusuma slide softly and a little
maid enters, bringing fanciful sweetmeats in
dishes of red and gold lacquer; kneeling to open
the fusuma and again to close them, for it is an
unpardonable breach of etiquette for a servant
to slide the screens standing; she glides away
only to return with tea and a tobacco box with
its cone of glowing charcoal in fine white ashes.
The silence is profound, and there is no sound
except, perhaps, the ripple of running water in
the garden without, or the splash of a leaping
carp in the pool, dark under overhanging azaleas,

or purple wistaria with its long racemes of flowers touching the surface of the water.

Finally the fusuma open and danna san is seen
kneeling and prostrating himself in courteous
greeting. He enters and, placing himself on the
cushion opposite, bows again with grave dignity
and inconceivable courtliness. The long formalities of a preliminary conversation are proceeded
with to the accompaniment of tea and pipes, and
presently, summoned by a clapping of hands, the
maids slide the fusuma and we pass through the
wide low corridors to the state apartments.
(Plate XXXVI.) Fusuma and shoji are wide
open and all along one side of the room lies some
magical garden, even though the house may be in
the midst of Tokyo or Kyoto.

One is seldom entertained in a private house,
the clubs and restaurants serve this purpose, for
there one can have amazing dinners with music
and geisha, but now and then specially favoured
mortals dine with my lord in his own residence.
Let us suppose this is to occur now. The master

claps his hands, the screens open, and several little maids appear, bringing little tables, covered with bowls of porcelain and lacquer. Facing each other, host and guest kneel on their cushions and the tables are arranged between them, the maids placing themselves on one side to be of instant service at any moment, and to fill little cups with hot, aromatic sake. Soups of many kinds, thin flakes of opalescent raw fish, eels, lobster, and fish of every kind and cooked in every way, follow each other in bewildering succession, and finally rice appears, served from a great lacquer box. Outside the garden is full of shifting light and subtle colour, here where we are sitting the room is spacious and airy and at every point the eye is refreshed by the most delicate detail, the most refined tone, the most perfect repose and reserve. Presently, at a gesture from the master, every vestige of the feast vanishes and we are left to smoke and talk, more intimately now and without the many formalities that are unavoidable at first.

XXXVI A Modern State Apartment in the Palace Style

XXXVII The Shukinro, Nagoya

When the time for departure arrives, the master himself comes to the door and servants assemble from every quarter to kneel on either side of the platform while host and guest face each other and bow again and again, murmuring the formal phrases of leave-taking, each of which is centuries old and breathes all the courtliness and dignity of a dead epoch, when feudalism was a vital and glorious institution. Shoes are resumed, the guest mounts into his kuruma, and as the circle of servants prostrate themselves, rolls away, bearing some gift commensurate with the rank of the host, and the more enduring memento of an unforgettable impression of refined living, courtesy, the product of immemorial centuries, and hospitality that is genuine in impulse, profoundly grateful to the Western recipient.

For the courtesy and simplicity of Japanese home life, the domestic architecture forms a faultless setting. It is absolutely frank and straightforward in construction, perfectly simple

in its forms, and reserved and refined in its
decorations; all the ornament is rigidly constructional, while the furnishings are of the simplest quality and only such as the nature of the
life demands. There is no ornament for the sake
of ornament, no woodwork or carving not de-
manded by the exigencies of construction, no
striving for picturesque effect through fantastic
irregularity, no overloading of unnecessary decoration, no confusion of furnishings, no litter of
trivial and embarrassing accessories. The spirit
of ornamented construction and no other ornament whatever that characterized Greek architecture finds its echo in Asia. As a result the effect
is more reserved, refined, gentlemanly, almost
ascetic, than is to be found elsewhere. No greater
contrast to our own fashion could be imagined.
With us the prime object appears to be the complete concealment of all construction of whatever
nature by an overlay of independent ornament.
With wainscot and marble and tiles, plaster, textiles, and paper-hangings, we create a perfectly

fictitious shell that masks all construction and exists quite independently of it.

We pile up our immutable little cells in super-imposed courses, cut narrow openings in the walls and fill them with flapping doors that are always in the way. We perforate the outer walls with awkward holes and fill them with plate-glass in order that we may gaze on a narrow back garden or a narrower street where nothing that is worth seeing ever occurs. With wainscot and drapery and paper-hangings we strive for an effect of protection and then nullify it by our plate-glass windows that afford only a garish light, and, in most cases, a view of things not worth looking at.

As a result the rooms are chilly and without sense of protection of winter, and stuffy and op-pressive in summer. The Japanese house is a revelation of the possibilities of exactly the oppo-site course. It is a permanent lesson in the value of simplicity, of modesty, of frankness, of natu-ralness in art.

In the inns and public houses of amusement we find the same qualities that mark the private house carried a little further. The form, the arrangement, the materials are the same, but with the greater size come also larger opportunities for artistic effects. The inns are almost always two stories high, never more, and the buildings enclose wonderful little courts surrounded by narrow galleries, or border on stone terraces and wandering gardens. There is one hotel at Uji that is a vision of delight, as it climbs along the high bank of a river, with its terraces crowded with blossoming, sweet-scented shrubs that lean over the mossy stone paths and crumbling steps. There is another wonderful inn at Hikone that was once the summer pavilion of the great Ii-Kamon-no-Kami, and its garden is famous throughout Japan. It is only one story high and rambles for an apparently illimitable distance up and down and away at surprising angles, its last outworks perched on the great wall over Lake Biwa, its scores of apartments opening on marvelous views that almost make one forget the beauty of the architectural surroundings. The Shukin-ro at Nagoya (Plate XXXVII) has no views, except of its own inimitable little courts, but it is the perfect type of a work of delicate art. All the true Japanese hotels are practically the same as a private house, so far as planning and construction are concerned, and in them a guest has the same privileges as in a dwelling, being at liberty to wander anywhere and even change his apartments every day if he like. In accordance with universal practice he eats, lives, and sleeps in the same rooms; if he prefers, and the inn is not crowded, he may choose any vacant room he pleases for his meals, or for his sleeping apartment.

The so-called " tea-houses " and restaurants are of course innumerable, for the Japanese, reserved, silent, even dogged when occasion demands, are by nature a gay and gregarious race, demanding relaxation and amusement and taking it frankly and simply at frequent intervals.

In general it is of the most innocent sort, flagrant immortality being no more prevalent than in any other type of modern civilization. Domestic etiquette holds the home a personal, even sacred possession, and except amongst the ultra-emancipated classes, a guest is seldom received there for any entertainment. For the high aristocracy, the many and exclusive clubs furnish the means of showing courtesy to the friend or the stranger, but the middle classes resort to hotels and restaurants, while the " tea-house " receives every one, high and low. A typical Japanese dinner in some exquisite restaurant on the edge of the river at Kyoto or overlooking the waters of Shinobazu in Tokyo, with delicate food, the music of samisen or koto, unearthly but bewitching songs and the magical dancing of silken geisha, is as bewildering an experience as usually falls to the lot of man. No less redolent of strange aloofness is rest and refreshment in some country or suburban tea-house draped with violet wistaria, showered by cherry petals, or half hidden in fan-

XXXVIII   A "Tea-house"

XXXIX A FARMHOUSE

tastic trees and smothering, blossoming shrubs
(Plate XXXVIII). Here the architecture is, of
course, of the simplest, as it is in the thatched
farmhouses that crowd every province of the
Empire (Plate XXXIX), but it is direct, spon-
taneous, ethnic, better in fact from the standpoint of art than some of the splendid new examples of an adapted " palace style " of building,
examples of which I have shown in Plates
XXXIII, XXXIV, XXXV, XXXVI.

In another and more ambiguous class of public houses the variation from the domestic type
is more marked, for they tend to pile themselves
up to the loftiest heights, even five and six stories
being not uncommon. In these there is usually
one great inner garden with hanging galleries
and dizzy bridges curving themselves across the
void from one side to another. At night when
the whole fabric glows with pale light through
latticed rice paper, and blood-red lanterns droop
from the gallery roofs, while the air is sweet with
the scent of flowers and full of the sound of

plashing fountains and the tinkling of samisen, the effect is almost unimaginably dreamy and poetic.

But whatever the nature of the structure the same qualities always express themselves. There is always a perfect frankness almost naïveté of plan; there is airiness and space and a constant variety of view, but quite without affectation or striving after effect; there is a faultless blending of subtle colours, a constant composition of delicate line and graceful form. Above all, there is a soul-reviving simplicity that is infinite in its dignity and reserve.

THE MINOR ARTS

At the close of the nineteenth century we stood as on a height of land whence we could look backward along the path of human development: a larger view, one more comprehensive and complete, was possible than ever before, and we were permitted to see many things, establish many relationships not recognized in the past. Amongst them was the position of art in its relation to what we are pleased to call civilization. The wider view we were then enabled to take gave, I think, something of a shock to our self-satisfaction, for we saw very clearly that the seventeenth, eighteenth, and nineteenth centuries had witnessed a steady and unbroken decline in all the arts but one, the art of music, and also that this decline, varying slightly in the periods of its duration, had extended over the entire world.

Retrogression there had been many times in the past, one or two or all the arts had suffered now and then and here and there, but the resulting inferiority had been relative always before; with us it was absolute. By this I mean that by the middle of the nineteenth century we had sunk to a point lower than ever in history, excepting only in music and in a measure in literature, but even here the loss was actual and measurable, for the great results achieved had been at the hands of isolated individuals and in spite of the general enmity of the great mass of the people. For the first time in the annals of the world art as an instinctive thing, as an heritage of humanity, had reached its term. We had sold our birthright, perhaps, though this is heresy, for a mess of pottage.

The consciousness of this startling condition came first to the few, and even before the nineteenth century had covered half its allotted course. These few began a feverish search through all the world for the vivifying flame that had flickered and died in the West. They

found it at the antipodes, in the then unravaged
East, and in one spot, in a little group of hermit
islands, in the most ancient and glorious King-
dom of Japan, they found it burning with yet
unhindered brightness and they announced their
treasure trove with exultation.

That was less than fifty years ago, but now
the flame has been extinguished also in this its
latest sanctuary, and the lamps hang empty of
oil and void of light.

In the history of the gradual extinction of the
artistic impulse Japan stands as the last of nations to forsake its heritage, as it also stands as
the first of the nations that now exist to assume
these rights and privileges of civilization. While
Europe was wallowing in the banalities of the
pagan Renaissance, insulting intelligence with
the architectural crudities of Palladio and Ma-
derna and the pictorial imbecilities of Guido
Reni and Salvator Rosa, Japan was building
the shrines of Nikko and painting the palace
temples of Kyoto with immortal decorations.

Later by two centuries, while the West was pro-
ducing black walnut and haircloth, plated silver
ice-pitchers, and chromo-lithographs, Japan was
quietly creating lacquers, cloisonné and embroideries, ivory carvings, screens and kakemono, any single example of which would honour
a contemporary museum of art. So also at the
beginning the architecture and sculpture of the
seventh and eighth centuries in Japan was in-
conceivably in advance of the rough brutalities
of the Western Europe of that time, then just
emerging from barbarism, and so it was to remain for almost five hundred years. The great
art of the West is comprised in three periods, one
of some three hundred years ending with. the
Christian era, one of a similar space of time dating from the reign of Justinian in the Eastern
Empire, and a third from the crusades to the
Reformation: the art of Japan lasts unbroken
from the middle of the seventh century to the
middle of the nineteenth, a duration of twelve
hundred years. It is, with that of Egypt, the

most prolonged art-record in the world, and though it passed through many vicissitudes, it never lapsed, remaining always vigorous and true. At different times it expressed itself through different modes, sculpture, architecture, painting, decoration, and " arts and crafts," each in turn serving its purpose as a vehicle of expression for a passion for beauty that never failed.

Japanese civilization begins with the year 552 when Korean missionaries brought from the mainland the vivifying spirit of a most exalted religious system, though actually the conversion of Shotoku Taishi, the Constantine of Japan, some forty years later, marks the permanent establishment of Buddhism, that noble union of religion and philosophy that was to be the inspiration of a civilization and an art destined to endure for almost thirteen hundred years. Art marked the birth of this great civilization as it marked its close, and the temples of Horiuji still stand in enduring record. The architect was a

Korean, and the style is the purest Chinese; Chinese also are the painted frescoes of the walls, with a slight Hindoo cast, and the superb sculptures, preserving, through all their orientalism, hints of Hellenic influence.

China has always been to Japan what Athens was to Rome; the first influence towards culture, learning and art came from her, and down even to the sixteenth century there was a constant reference to her on every subject. She remained the perfect standard in letters, philosophy, religion, sculpture, architecture, painting, and music, but she was always a guide, not a model for narrow copying. The germ of every phase of civilization emanated from her, but these germs developed independently, and as a result, while Japan never quite won to the astounding height of perfect development that was achieved in Hangchow in the twelfth century, she yet produced a more persistent and lasting culture than was granted to her great mother.

All the art of Japan is therefore primarily

Chinese, but it is marked by a certain searching vitality, a mobility and an almost nervous
eagerness that are all her own. As I have said, the
first architecture, painting, sculpture, and poetry
were Chinese or Sino-Korean, but almost immediately, so fertile was the soil, so powerful
the impulse of Buddhism, native Japanese arose
to carry on the work and on their own lines.
The unknown architect of the Yakushiji pagoda
was undoubtedly a Japanese. Tori Busshi,
though of Chinese blood in part, was born in
Japan early in the seventh century and was the
first of the great sculptors, while Akahito and
Hitomaru, who flourished about the year 700,
were the first of the famous poets. Kose-no-
Kanaoka was the first of the painters; he was
much later in time, living during the second half
of the ninth century. Komachi, a third great
poet, was his contemporary. An hundred years
later came Eshin and Jocho, sculptors, and
Murasaki Shikibu, the first and greatest of the
novelists of Japan.

All these were products of the great Fujiwara period, the first essentially Japanese manifestation of governmental possibilties. The old and primitive patriarchal system had been reorganized on the Chinese bureaucratic plan in the year 600, but seventy years later the Fujiwara family usurped almost all of the sovereign power and remained dominant for four hundred years. This was artistically a period of architecture, sculpture, and poetry, and the results were amazing in their perfection. The sculpture of Japan is almost unknown, but Horiuji, Nara, and Kyoto bear witness to the fact that it ranks with the most perfect in the world; in point of finely studied line it has no superior outside of Greece. Nearly all the Fujiwara architecture has perished but the exquisite Ho-o-do of Byodo-in still remains a marvel of refinement of proportion and exquisite decoration.

Following the fall of the house of Fujiwara came a long period of political anarchy when the rival houses of the Taira and Minomoto struggled for the mastery. During this epoch architecture contrived to develop, but the other major arts languished, nor did they regain any degree of brilliancy under the Hojo Shogun. Towards the middle of the fourteenth century the Shogunate passed into the hands of the house of Ashikaga, and with the beginning of the fifteenth century came the great burst of artistic genius that, after the early sculpture of the first years, is the great esthetic glory of Japan. Josetsu was the first of the great school of painters, Chodensu its most famous representative, and these immortals were quickly followed by Sesshu, one of the greatest landscape painters of all time, Shubun, and Kano Motonobu, the first of a famous line and a decorative artist almost without a rival. Unkei was meanwhile restoring the glories of the Chinese and Fujiwara sculpture. In the second generation came Iwasa Matahei, Kano Eitoku, and Kano Sanraku. Then the Napoleonic Hideyoshi strode on the stage, overturning the foundations of all established systems, and when he passed like a dying meteor the Tokugawa family assumed the Shogunate.

Now came a change, though painting still remained the chosen mode of artistic expression. For a time Korin and the later painters of the Kano family preserved the classical traditions of the Ashikaga school, but in 1750 Okyo and his great pupil Sosen founded the Shijo school of avowed realists and fixed the popular style that was to continue to the end.

In the meantime how had fared the artist-crafts, the art, that is, of all the people, the art that was the sign of joy in life and industrial vitality, and the proof of the depth to which the current civilization had permeated?

Well we know that from the very first whatever had been made by any workman had been beautiful. Of course much, nearly all, indeed, that dates from the earliest period, has perished. We know that the arts of the potter, the weaver, and the metal worker had come from China with

the sixth-century missionaries, and for the following eight centuries had followed the progress
of the major arts closely and intimately. But
when feudalism became an established system
at the beginning of the thirteenth century, then
came the opportunity of the minor arts, and under the Ashikaga these developed to such a degree that they themselves actually became major
arts; lacquer, porcelain, cloisonné, wood carving, screen painting, embroidery, goldsmithery,
metal working, ivory carving, each and all became exalted to a marvelous height, and remained there until the end of the old régime.

The art of Japan falls easily into four great
periods: first, the Chinese and Fujiwara epoch
lasting from 600 to 1100, when the chosen arts
in their order of precedence were sculpture,
poetry, and architecture; second, the Kamakura period, when architecture alone maintained
and even increased its glory: this kind of inter-
regnum lasted three hundred years, from 1100
until 1400; third, the Ashikaga epoch, the golden

age of art when painting became unrivaled in its perfection while sculpture and the industrial arts followed close behind; fourth, the Tokugawa régime, when architectural decoration, together with the industrial arts, leaped to the front in a blaze of unexampled glory, architecture showing signs of decadence, and painting suffering from the realism that the followers of the Shijo school exaggerated into a prominence that would have shocked its founders. Then Commodore Perry opened the ports, and like a house of cards the marvelous dream-fabric crumbled into ruin. The Shogunate was abolished in 1868, feudalism was destroyed in 1871, the wearing of swords was prohibited in 1876, in 1889 the Mikado promulgated the Constitution, and a civilization that had endured for thirteen centuries, a civilization that had produced a national character of singular nobility and an art of almost unexampled beauty, passed away forever. Japanese art is now history; as a vital and contemporary power it has no existence.

I am supposed to write of the Arts and Crafts
of Japan, but if by this is meant a certain few of
the minor arts of a people, the task is an impossible one, for in this sense the arts and crafts do
not exist in Japan; there was never really any
distinction between the major and the minor
arts, a poem, a devotional picture, a statue, a
temple is just as much a piece of craftsmanship
as a netuske, or a lacquer box, and a carved
ramma or a bronze incense koro is just as much
a vehicle of the highest esthetic and spiritual expression as a kakemono by Cho-densu or the Dai
Butsu of Kamakura. It was all art; that is, the
achievement of the highest visual beauty, the
expression of joy in life and exultation in well-
doing, and the communication of spiritual and
emotional enthusiasm. Art is simply the symbolical expression of otherwise inexpressible
ideas, and the Japanese, living in a beautiful
land, inspired by an exalted form of religion,
and ultimately ennobled by a splendid feudalism
that enhanced every inborn trait of honour and

chivalry, simply did this better than almost any other people in the world. Art should be at least the voicing of health, joy, the delight in work, and the conviction of a beautiful religious faith. When conditions are such that all the people are blessed with the possession of these things, then the arts and crafts will flourish, and no hard line will divide them from what are called the major arts.

In Japan every man, whether he were daimyo, samurai, or peasant, lived practically out of doors all the time and all the year round, he bathed at least three times a day, and, except at the luxurious close of the Kamakura period when tea-drinking and incense-burning ceremonies tended to produce sloth and effeminacy, every man was active and vigorously busy. Under feudalism this vitality of action became characteristic of the entire race, and as a result there were universal health and perfect joy in life. Japan has always been either an absolute monarchy, a powerful aristocracy, or a splendid feudalism; therefore the principles of law and order — except during the Kamakura anarchy — have always been universally accepted, and honour, faithfulness, and personal devotion have been supreme. As a result there was an unusually high standard of government and industry of all kinds flourished, so there was general content and a greater continuity of good civil conditions than can easily be found during any similar period in Europe. Finally Buddhism was supreme and its noble ethical system, its profound philosophy, and its intense religious quality worked together to build up strong character and to incite the imagination and the emotions of the people to the highest pitch.

No other result than that which actually followed could be predicated from these conditions: namely, a kind of life, a mode of thought, a quality of action that made artistic expression inevitable. For art of any kind is not a commodity, it cannot be bought and sold, it is a result that follows inevitably from certain conditions, and these conditions held in Japan for thirteen centuries as they held in medieval Europe for three centuries. The Japanese were clean, brave, honourable, religious, loyal, and art followed like the blossom and fruitage of a tree.

The minor arts, like the major arts, were simply the proper expression, as I have said, of a healthy delight in doing everything just as well as it could possibly be done. Buddhism, chivalry, and unflinching loyalty to the King and to the dead all taught the lesson of faithfulness in small things as well as great. Whatever any workman did, he did as well as it could possibly be done. Ugliness was then, as it is now, a sin; carelessness and cheapness of workmanship were then, as they are now, a crime. The fact that a thing was humble in its function was no reason why it should not be perfect in form and fashioning. The Japanese knew that art was not an amenity of life, a mere prettiness, pleasing, perhaps, but decidedly a luxury; they knew that it was the mark of the man, the proof of his character, the pledge of his culture, and therefore they were ashamed to do anything that was not beautiful. This is really all there is to be said about Japanese arts and crafts. The forms are new to us, the methods singular, the patterns strange and foreign, but these qualities are superficial. Essentially there is no difference but one of degree between the arts of Japan and those of medieval Europe. Unbroken civilization, a continuity of tradition, and an absence of religious heresies resulted in training the eye and the hand of the Japanese artisan to a point never attained by his brothers of the West; but the impulse, the motive was the same, and it is this impulse that must be incited again if we are ever to attain once more proficiency in the arts.

I said in the beginning that with the close of the last century we stood on an eminence from which we could obtain a general view of the recent past impossible to us before. In this view lies a certain space so arid, so desolate, that in a way it cuts us off from the ancient tradition that is ours by right. The second and third quarters of the nineteenth century will stand forever as a kind of Babylonish Captivity, an epoch of horror that isolates us from the past. During that time we sank lower in industrial art, in the art of the race, than ever before in recorded history, and as a result the mental attitude of the world was seriously changed. We have simply to start all over again, and by the grace of God we will start properly with the industrial arts; but we cannot start from them immediately, we must achieve first of all the industrial, economic, political, and spiritual conditions that will result inevitably in some form of artistic expression. How we are to do this is not for me to say, but it must be done, for if we do not express ourselves artistically in all we do, then we are barbarians.

In a curious old book written during the reign of Queen Victoria by Sir Rutherford Alcock, I find this delicious estimate of Japanese art:

" There is much, especially in the province of

art properly so called, to which the Japanese
cannot make the slightest pretension. They cannot produce by an effort works to be compared
with the noble specimens of repoussé carving
from the chisel of a Vechte, a Morel Ladeuil, or
a Monti, which the great International Exposition showed: yet the Japanese bronze castings
are, some of them, scarce inferior in skilled
workmanship and mixture of metals to anything
we can produce of the same kind. No Japanese
can produce anything to be named in the same
day with a work from the pencil of a Landseer,
a Roberts, or a Stanfield, a Lewis, or a Rosa
Bonheur."

To compare the " repoussé artists " Vechte
and Morel Ladeuil, whoever they may have
been, with Okyo and Hidari Jingoro, and Roberts and Lewis with Sesshu and Kano Motonobu,
would be idiotic were it not so laughable; but
poor Sir Rutherford will serve very well to show
how truly we had sunk in the middle of the century into the pit of perfect barbarism. Later the

worthy Englishman tells us why the Japanese are so inferior to Vechte and Morel Ladeuil. He says, " I should say that there was a material civilization of a high order in which all the industrial arts had been brought to as great perfection as could well be obtainable without the aid of steam power and machinery."

I have quoted thus at length from the admirable Briton just to show how great are our grounds for encouragement today. Forty years ago nine men out of ten would have agreed with him, today he would stand alone. We know now that steam power and machinery may destroy but that they cannot create art, and this is the first battle; but there is yet another and a greater fight that must be won before the way is clear before us, and that is the fight against the heresy that we can have art at any time if we are willing to pay for it, in other words, that art is a commodity, not a result. Some years ago the Arts and Crafts movement began in England: a little later its results were the only truly good industrial art in the Western world. Today the movement has spread all over the Continent with deplorable results, and in England itself exaggeration, affectation, and artificiality are taking the place of the first true arts and crafts. The art nouveau of France and Belgium is worse than haircloth and black walnut, and Birmingham and Grand Rapids are making arts and crafts furniture by " steam power and machinery." [1]

We are building on shifting sands, we are beginning at the top, not the bottom, and we are playing with a pack of cards. Japan teaches us one lesson besides that of the inefficiency of steam power as an incentive to art, and that lesson is that healthy living and joyful labour, just economic conditions, good government, a chivalric mind, a fine sense of honour, and a deep religious faith must come first as the rocky base whereupon we may build our fabric of noble art.

[1] And what in God's Name shall we say of its successor, the " Modernist " work of today?

A COLOUR PRINT OF YEIZAN

With some thoughts on Japanese painting

" IT is necessary to exercise the understanding in
painting, or, as it were, to carry the mind at the point
of the brush. To introduce too much is commonplace,
and the artist must exercise his judgment in omitting
everything superfluous or detrimental to the attainment of his object. It is the fault of foreign pictures
that they dive too deeply into realities and preserve
too many details that were better suppressed. Such
works are but as groups of words. The Japanese
picture should aspire to be a poem of form and
colour." (From an eighteenth century Japanese essay on painting.)

　　·　　·　　·　　·　　·　　·　　·　　·

" Amongst pictures is a kind called naturalistic, in
which it is considered proper that flowers, grasses,
fishes, insects, etc., should bear exact resemblance to
nature. This is a special style and must not be depre-
ciated, but as its object is merely to show forms,
neglecting the rules of art, it is commonplace and

without taste. In ancient pictures the study of the art of outline and of the laws of taste was respected without attention to close imitation of form." (Shuzan, 1777.)

This is not a masterpiece by some giant of the fifteenth century: it is signed by no Sesshu, Korin, or Motonobu: it is a cheap coloured print struck from wooden blocks in the XVIIIth century, but it says much, perhaps all we can ever understand, of the pictorial art of Japan.

.   .   .   .

Art is absolute beauty: without this there is no art. It is also much more, but this is the beginning, even if it is not the end. What absolute beauty is, Western philosophy does not define, but sane civilization has always recognized it, even if intellectual demonstration has been wanting. Why one line, or combination of lines, should be beautiful, another repulsive; why one musical phrase should be exalting, another debasing; why one colour composition should satisfy absolutely, another repel — these are

XL A Colour-print of Yeizan

mysteries not even St. Thomas Aquinas can solve. A Bodenhausen Madonna and a Japanese kakemono; an aria from Rigoletto, and the " Good Friday Spell " from Parsifal; Bernini and Praxiteles; antitheses, yet why?

The philosophy of the East gives a hint; absolute beauty is dual in its nature: mystical manifestation, through unconscious but inevitable selection from myriad lives (forgotten yet operative), of the failures that were partial only, and that therefore through process of selection and discrimination become visible evidences of the best thus far achieved. The best, not of one life, but of millions; higher, therefore, than the best of one. Karma, in a way, yet a Karma that is always good, for it is not humans alone who weave this cord of destiny, but all nature, animate or (as we call it) inanimate: all mental and spiritual forces, art as much as you or I. Also is it, in another aspect, mystical foreknowledge of the final Absolute to which we all are tending through incarnation and reincarnation; not only the subliminal composite of the good of all the past, but a leaping on by force of achievement to heights yet unachieved; Karma and Beatific Vision in one. So beauty is something that never was in the past, nor is now, but shall be hereafter, the last residuum from the winnowing of experience illuminated by the aura even of Nirvana itself.

We may or may not accept the solution of Eastern mysticism: the fact remains that beauty, absolute, never was, and is not now, and is to be found neither in nature nor in art. If in either of these a thing is discovered which seems absolutely beautiful, the fact of discovery proves that it is not absolute, but partial only, and therefore to be accepted merely as material from which beauty by psychological or mystical processes may be evolved. In other words, what we call nature is no more perfect than man himself, but is constantly developing, and imitation or copying of nature is not the registering of beauty, but of the imperfect. Art, therefore, being at least the record of the search for absolute beauty, must, if it is good, avoid the replication of natural facts, since these are in themselves beautiful only in a transitory and ephemeral way.

Beauty, then, which we may call the Intimation of the Absolute, is the first requisite of all art. In this respect nine tenths of all modern " art " fails completely; it is imitation, ingenuity, photography, a record of objective and sociological and psychological data — what you will — but it is not art in any true and universal sense.

In the pictorial arts beauty is of many kinds: beauty of line, form, colour, light and dark, space composition. You may grow weary searching through the Luxembourg, or any Salon or Academy exhibition before you find a picture possessing all, or even one of these primary notes of true art: you cannot take up a common colour-print made in Japan before 1880 that does not show them all.

Again, art is good workmanship, the perfect adaption of means to an end; no boggling with uncertainties, no prodigality of effort, everything direct, instantaneous: such workmanship as that of which Velasquez was supreme master, and Michelangelo and John Sargent. Here every Japanese painter is master. Note in the print the swift, sure lines of the scroll, the curves of the sleeves of the woman's gown. The hand of a Japanese is trained like the hand of a clever surgeon, his eye like that of a master mariner, his brain answers as instantly and clearly as that of a great general.

Finally, art is the manifestation of the unattained, the communication of the inexpressible. Without sacrilege, we may say that it partakes of the nature of a Sacrament; it is both a symbol and a medium between the finite, the conditioned, and the infinite, the unconditioned. To revert again to Eastern philosophy, the mind, physical in its nature, deals with those things that fall within the span of a single life, it is built up of experience, of the happenings between the cradle and the grave, it records no more, it can express no more: it is a physical function and this only. But in the second place there is a superior mind, a sublimated consciousness, that is the concatenation of myriads of incarnations. It is an attribute of the inextinguishable Karma, it is to the physical mind what man is to the mollusk. In it are fixed to all eternity the records of an infinite past, the seeds of an infinite future. To it are added, life by life, all that is precious and of moment in a sequence of existences. It is the source in man of all imagination, dreams, and visions; of aspirations and exaltations; of honour, self-sacrifice, devotion; of love, poetry, and religion. We may, if we like, call it the immortal soul.

Therefore it is the essential element in man. Art of every kind is its most facile means of expression, and while art as art may exist independently of its function as a mode of supermundane expression and inter-communication, it finds, nevertheless, its highest manifestation in this unearthly and symbolical language.

Man is a plexus of aggregated individuals, yet he has two general natures corresponding to the dual mind; the one that is the physical product of a single existence, the other that is the concentration of millions thereof. The language of the first is the ordinary spoken and written language of a people, that of the second is art.

．　．　．　．　．　．　．　．

What, it may be said, has all this tenuous theorizing to do with a colour-print by Yeizan? We of the West, who in looking at a picture search for its qualities of truth to facts as we know them — facts of nature, facts of history; who are taught that correct anatomy is the first requisite in figure drawing, correct archæology in historical work, correct delineation of character in portraiture — we, on turning suddenly to a Japanese print or kakemono, find nothing of these at first, and argue, therefore, ignorance on the part of the painter. The photograph and the anatomical chart being our criteria, we find at first nothing but grotesqueness and wilful disregard of patent facts. In other words, we have Muybridged our minds until artistic perception is no longer possible.

For actually great Japanese painting possesses all the elements named above; it is in a greater or less degree, varying with the painter, an approach to absolute beauty, of line and line-composition, of colour and colour-composition, of design and of space-composition. Also, in a greater or less degree, it approaches technical perfection. The Kano did not

> " splash at a ten-league canvas
>   With brushes of comets' hair,"

but they did, so far as was possible to man, achieve complete directness, instantaneous certainty. They knew to an hair's breadth what they were to do, and exactly how they were to set about doing it. The space covered is comparatively small, but in the sure spring and exact touching of the goal Michelangelo himself could

not better them. Finally, there is every reason
to believe that in the highest reaches of art, in
subtle reminder and re-creation of the accumulated past forbidden to earthly memory, and in
the dim foreshadowing of a future equally forbidden to the physical mind, the painters of
Japan far excel those of our own race whom we
can know and understand — Leonardo, Gior-
gione, Botticelli, Dürer, Rossetti. I say there is
every reason to believe this, for actually we cannot know, we of the West to whom they of the
East are as of another planet.

In so far as beauty is in itself a showing
forth, and an incentive to, mystical memory of
accumulated experience, either of the individual
or the race, Japanese art is operative in our own
case. When, after long study of a picture or a
print, we begin to see how every line, every space,
every composition of line, *notan,* form, and colour is in itself beautiful, then we feel that unmistakable thrill, that wistful call from the abyss
of the forgotten that declares the half awakening

of the mysterious power, ourselves, yet more than ourselves, that hears the cry of the universal and answers, half believing yet half afraid.

But for that other attribute of art, the prophecy of the Beatific Vision, here we are on different ground. Leonardo we can understand, and Wagner, and Browning. They speak our tongue though through different arts. But the Japanese painters speak in a language and to a consciousness whereof we have neither part nor parcel. Therefore, we can only assume and believe their art to be at least equal to our own in this respect; the tangible proof is wanting, and must ever remain so.

Yet even omitting this, we have enough left on which we may found a judgment of Japanese pictorial art. How much of the painting of our own race becomes a vehicle rather than an end in itself? Not one in an hundred painters assumes the prophetic office, not one in ten of the pictures of those that do is in any sense a revelation: yet the art is good if it is really art, and to be this it must be an expression of absolute beauty, and, if possible, a manifestation of masterly craft as well.

The pictorial art of Japan possesses these two qualities in the highest degree. Pure beauty is a prerequisite, good workmanship an almost unfailing accompaniment. For a time there was an attempt on the part of many to discriminate against Japanese painting as " decorative " and therefore not pictorial. This was necessary if we were to retain a few shreds of admiration for the vast mass of modern painting which possesses no single element of beauty and is in no sense " decorative." It was supposed to be art, however, hence the discrimination. Now, as a matter of fact, every great picture of the past has been primarily " decorative." If it had not been, it could never have ranked as a great picture. Tintoretto's " Marriage of Bacchus and Ariadne," Michelangelo's Sistine ceiling, Botticelli's " Spring," Titian's " Sacred and Profane Love," Rembrandt's " Night Watch," these and

an hundred other masterpieces are such because
they are " decorative," in other words, are masterpieces of pure beauty, either of drawing, composition, colour, or of all of these qualities. Each
has many other splendid attributes, but it is not
the anatomical power of Michelangelo's bodies,
the atmosphere of Titian's golden dream, the
vital character in Rembrandt's heads, nor yet
his mastery of the mysteries of light, that make
the pictures great: it is simply and only that
they are all manifestations of beauty in some of
its noblest modes: all things else are but acts of
supererogation, or at best added virtues that are
cumulative in their import.

The beauty of a Kano Motonobu, a Sesshu,
a Korin, is essentially the same, the beauty in
this print of Yeizan is close kin to the beauty in
a Filippo Lippi or a Bernardino Luini: the spacing of the lights and darks, the composition, the
individual and combined lines, the sheer beauty
of form in each separate part, all are infinitely
studied, perfectly competent, final as far as they

go. A Giovanni Bellini may appeal to us more, and it certainly should, for it is of our own race, but this is an accident of blood and has no bearing on the quality of the work in the abstract.

Again, we stand in awe before the technique of Velasquez, Tintoretto, Sargent, and well we may: they are past masters of paintercraft, but so are the Japanese; the same test that justifies them of the West vindicates them of the East: it is one impulse, one genius, one achievement.

I am not arguing that the arts of Japan, and the pictorial arts in particular, should appeal to us as does the art of our own race: the gulf between East and West is impassable. The sculptors of Greece, the painters of Italy, the builders of France and England, were men of our own race, their history is ours, their tongue our tongue. No other art can possibly be to us as this which is our own, but if we isolate ourselves in our Western insolence, denying, for example, the name of art to all pictures not painted in oil or tempera, on panels or canvas, and framed

in carved and gilded wood, then we stamp ourselves barbarians, shut ourselves away from the
possibility of an esthetic experience not to be
found elsewhere. Nor is condescending patron-
age a whit less virtuous. " A very high type of
artistic production indeed, for an Asiatic race."
" Admirable decoration, perhaps the very best,
but hardly what one would call pictorial, or High
Art." " Wonderful artisans no doubt, with a
marvelous sense of the decorative, but curiously
limited in their knowledge of anatomy, modeling, and perspective." Phrases such as these are
worse than a frank and brutal denying of the
very name of art to the work of the painters of
the great Japanese schools.

Asiatic civilization was for some centuries the
highest to be found on earth. There is no " High
Art " that is not permanently decorative. If any
quality of anatomy, modeling, or perspective
has been banished from a Japanese picture, it is
merely because this quality, perfectly well un-
derstood by the painter, has been deleted simply

because it was not necessary to the attainment of the end in view. These are the replies to the three strictures quoted above.

Come back again to the colour-print (Plate XL): what would it have gained had the head been modeled like a crayon drawing from the cast; had the bones declared themselves through the muscles, the muscles through the gown; had the figure been bathed in accidental lights and had it stood before us surrounded by atmosphere, a wonder of perspective? Nothing, so far as pure beauty is concerned, for this lies in its rhythm of line, in its calm, clear spaces, in its juxtaposition of lights and darks. The elements it lacks may be assembled to produce equal beauty, the point is that they are not the only Divinely ordained means whereby this may be attained. The East has found others of equal potency; the result, the manifestation of absolute beauty in visible form, is the same.

The object, then, of the Japanese painter is the attainment of pure beauty. To him, nourished as his fathers before him for unnumbered generations, on the fundamental doctrine that thought, will, desire, the universe itself, all are illusion, all visible and tangible things are no more than the emanation of rudimentary mind, therefore utterly imperfect and unworthy of perpetuation. He does not search far and wide for a fairer type of face or form, a nobler natural prospect. He does not ransack his memory or his sketch-books for notes of pose, gesture, accessories: his pictures are not built up of beautiful elements gathered from many sources and through long periods. This is the method of the West — is now at all events, in the case of such work as possesses any claim whatever to the qualities of true art. Instead he takes any subject, however outwardly commonplace, and then applies to it three processes: Selection, Emphasis, Idealization.

Almost instinctively he chooses the essential lines, elements, and qualities, throwing all else away. Of these he lays stress on those that play into his hand for beauty, minimizing the others, and then, either, as we should say, by the exercise of his infallible good taste, or, as he would say, controlled by that mystical elder memory that tests all things by the standards established through myriads of forgotten lives, he goes on to translate his chosen details into terms of the beautiful.

Here we return to the first proposition in this, I fear, incoherent essay — that the nature of Absolute Beauty is undemonstrable outside the mazes of Oriental psychology and metaphysics. Yet whatever it is, the Japanese attains it. In painting, as in architecture and in the earlier sculpture, beauty is as omnipresent as it is in the art of Greece and that of the Middle Ages in Europe. Yet it is absolutely impossible to demonstrate this fact in words. If any one can show clearly and scientifically just why St. Mark's is beautiful, the Panthéon hideous, he will do well; yet there is the fact, and here is the fact of consummate beauty in Japanese painting.

And it is this that is all-important. The art of Japan is the art of pure beauty. How achieved, and why, are questions beside the mark. We may by careful study discern wherein this beauty lies; in what kind of lines and what combinations of lines; in what spacing of lights and darks, in what systems of rhythm, echo, and development, in what arrangements and combinations of colour. We may even discover the underlying laws, if they exist, but for my own part, I am inclined to think that these laws can never be formulated in terms comprehensible by man. Art does not exist by law, at all events by law man-made or uttered by man. It is an inevitable result: if it exists, good; if it is absent no power on earth aimed at its direct creation will avail in the smallest degree.

And here follows, as a moral, the story of the Chinese painter, Wu tao-tsz.

.   .   .   .

"Lord," said Wu tao-tsz, prostrating himself, "my labour is at an end."

The King regarded him with scant favour. "Behold," he said, "how the curtain that has hung before the wall of my palace, hiding all sign of your work, still insults my vision. Will you deign to remove it?"

"Even so, Lord," and at a touch the curtain sank to the ground.

The King started, then stood silent gazing on the wonder before him. It seemed that the wall of the palace had melted away, and in its place was a wide window giving on a land such as no man in earthly life had ever seen before. A wall of pale jade, intricately wrought, lay in front, pierced by a gleaming doorway of coral lacquer and closed by gates of chiseled gold. And above, reaching off into limitless distance, lay a radiant country of trees and flowers, with cascades of silver water, mountains of marvelous shapes, and clouds like visible dreams. Temples of ivory, amethyst, and gold flamed in the amber air, and for a moment the King believed he could hear faint chanting and mystical music, scent the perfumes of unknown incense mingling with the odour of rose gardens and jasmine. Finally he spoke.

" You have done well, Wu tao-tsz, for you have painted, not this earth, but the very heaven of heavens that is the emanation of the Lord Buddha."

" Not so, Lord," and the painter prostrated himself once more. " This that you see, you have seen before, but only as you have seen the single dew-drops which, gathered together, become the immeasurable sea. This is but the veil of what shall be, a poor symbol of the smile of the Ineffable One. Beyond — "

He knelt, prostrating himself now before the gates. Then in a breath they swung open. Wall, gates, portal dissolved and faded away and for one instant of time lay revealed a land of such wonder and majesty that the vision Wu tao-tsz had wrought seemed but a mean and sordid desolation. The King fell to the ground covering his face with his sleeve, but before his eyeballs were seared by the glory of the Utterly Forbidden, he saw Wu tao-tsz rise and pass into the Vision of the Absolute, saw him melt into the unspeakable radiance of the smile of the Blessed One.

When, after long abasement, he ventured to raise his eyes, the gates were closed, nor when he touched them were they other than painted silk.

And Wu tao-tsz no man saw ever again on earth.

A NOTE ON JAPANESE SCULPTURE

OF all forms of artistic activity in this most artistic and active of lands, I suppose sculpture is really the least known, the least considered, except in so far as the term might be applied to the work of the industrial artists, the many and nameless masters of the minor arts. Yet in actuality the sculpture of Japan, the plastic or chiseled work, that is, which possesses the universal elements of monumental art, is at least as noble and admirable and as worthy high place beside the achievements of Western art, as are the painting and the industrial arts whose position is now so nearly assured.

We admit at last that the Japanese schools of painting are worthy of equal honour with those of the Early Renaissance in Europe: the racial impulse and the religion were different and the results are widely sundered in their superficial aspects, nevertheless we know now that the supreme tests of great painting may be applied as safely to the pictures of Cho-densu, Shubun, and Kano Motonobu as to those of Leonardo, Botticelli, and the Bellini. We are beginning to appreciate the fact that Japanese architecture is not a sport of Asiatic barbarism, but a style as logical, articulate, and highly developed as those of Greece and France and England. Of the major arts sculpture alone is left out of the reckoning. Mention the word and nine out of ten men will think at once of the Daibutsu of Kamakura and the Ni-o that scowl at one from the main gates of the Buddhist temples — nothing more. Every one is impressed by the sacred solemnity of the gray-green Presence in the Kamakura valley, every one is delighted by the grotesque violence and the savage exaggeration of the Deva Kings, but few stop to analyze artistic elements of the great Buddha, and still fewer realize that back of the threat-

XLI KOREAN STATUE, NARA

ening wardens of the gates stretches a line of sculptured masterpieces reaching even to the sixth century of the Christian era.

Nevertheless this is the case; some day a man will come who will penetrate the dusty gloom of Horiuji, Horinji, Todaiji, Kofukuji and all the other treasure houses of central Japan, dragging into the light the wonderful examples of sculpture hidden there, search these lines and masses, point out their qualities of everlasting nobility, and add to human knowledge another — indeed several other — immortal schools of sculpture.

For my own part, I have only peered for a moment into these forgotten shrines, brushed a little dust from odd statues here and there, gathered — I fear by stealth and the doubtfully justifiable generosity of some good Japanese friends — a few poor and faded photographs of two or three out of scores of works of art utterly unknown except to Japanese students.

The impression is lasting, however, and

prompts a few random notes, not as a contribution to the sum of knowledge of this so little known field of Japanese art, but only, if it may be, to pique the curiosity of others and so lead them to search still further into a field that promises much.

Earliest in point of times is a bronze figure formerly in Horiuji but now in the Nara Museum (Plate XLI). It is of the sixth century: pure Korean, or, if not that, then the earliest of all Japanese work and executed under Korean orders. In any case, it is Korean in style, and absolutely priceless to any student of the historical development of art. It is a strange, sexless figure, tall and slim, mysterious and baffling to a degree. The drapery is formalized and decorative, conventionalism raised to the nth power, but the type and the modeling of the head and hands are almost classical. The pose too. while reserved and formal, has yet a certain suave grace that is most appealing. There are an hundred reasons why this Korean figure is absolutely invaluable. Not only is it a fine type of pure and law-abiding sculpture, full of beauty and spiritual calm, but it is a priceless example of that amazing Asiatic modification of an Hellenic norm which proves a ramification of classic influence, a persistent survival of the Greek idea, in lands and among people severed from the primal source by almost the whole diameter of being.

The influence of Athens on the art of Asia was as great as in the case of Medieval Europe, and the man who will undertake to trace the devious course of this influence from Hellas across the whole width of Asia will have a new field full of great possibilities. He will also have the certainty of a tedious task, for of the myriad connecting links between Phidias and Tori Busshi nearly all have perished. Persia, India, China, and Korea have been swept clean of artistic records, and if we may judge from this single statue in Nara the loss is irreparable. What must have been the art of China, for example, during the first centuries of the Christian era, if a thing like this came to a mission station in a comparatively barbarous land from a country that was not the source of civilization, but only a recent triumph of missionary enterprise on the part of China herself, the great mother of civilizations?

Again in this work we see the models on which Japan was to build her art of national sculpture, as in the monastery of Horiuji we see the prototype of her architecture. This sixth-century work in and around Nara is the beginning of the art of Japan, and its value is correspondingly great.

A century later Tori Busshi begins the great line of Japanese sculptors, though himself of Chinese descent and Chinese or Korean training. In his work and that of his seventh-century school, we find exactly what we should have expected: conventionalism, or rather formalism, carried into every part of the work, into the body as well as into the vesture; at the same

XLII AN AMIDA OF THE SEVENTH CENTURY

XLIII   A Seventh-Century Bodhisatwa

time an access of decorative quality in line and mass. Except in the exquisite formalism of the drapery little classical feeling remains, and even its vestiges have taken on a cast as Oriental as the faces and figures. As studies of line, pure and consummate, I know few things in sculpture more nearly ultimate than these seventh-century statues of Horiuji and Yakushiji. (Plates XLII and XLIII.)

With the eighth century we come at a bound into an era of Japanese sculpture, national, ethnic, perfectly developed. The first formalism has worked itself out, traditions have been discounted so far as their accidents are concerned. Japan has found herself and announces that fact in perfectly audible phrases. In religious sculpture these traditions still persist, the composition and the lines of the drapery hark back to the early Korean or rather Asiatic mode, the faces have stupefied into conventional expressionlessness: dogma is steadily conservative. On the other hand, even in official sculpture, here and there the bonds are breaking, a certain realism is creeping into the poses and the details, while now and again in the faces, character, typical and unmistakable, begins to show itself. More or less portrait statues begin to appear in the shape of apotheosized warriors and incarnations of heroism and force, and here we come at once into a full-fledged school of vital sculpture. Figures such as those in Plate XLIV are the very embodiment of force, with power and ability in every line. Consider the poise and dash of such a splendid, sinewy thing as the Incarnation of War, the spring and sweep of the body, the tensity of nerve, the howling savagery of the distorted face conventionalized like a Greek mask; or again, the rigid alertness, the power, concentrated and controlled, in Plate XLV. In all of these the bodies are fully articulated, the faces, particularly the last, unmistakably portraits, yet portraits that are more than the effigies of individuals, they are amalgamations of a race, manifestations of national character.

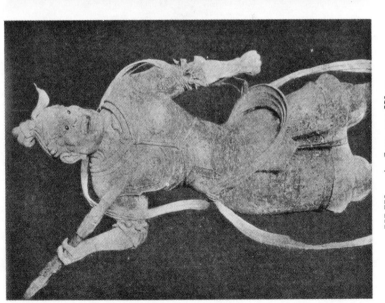

XLIVb A Sculptured Guardian

XLIVa A God of War

XLV Incarnation of Power

Note also the superb armour, almost classical in its lines, without fantasticism or exaggeration, clean-cut, splendid in line, noble in its surface. These are great statues, all of them, works of the highest art: nothing better was ever produced in Europe after the fall of Rome. Plate XLVI*a*, also, is a wonder of portraiture, indeed I doubt if anything more full of individuality and character has ever been wrought than these last two heads of the eighth century in Japan.

All the work thus far considered has been of the Nara period; of the Kyoto period, which covered the next four centuries until 1192, I have been able to obtain no photographs of the work of the earlier years, but of the tenth century we have such keenly characteristic work as the two portrait studies in Plates XLVI*b* and XLVII*a;* one of a Buddhist priest, the other of a young daimyo. In these we find the same intensity of personality, together with a progressive development of Japanese qualities, both racial and artistic. The little noble in particular is a perfect masterpiece of sculpture, intimate in character, real to a degree, both in type and detail, decorative in its arrangement of line and the minutiæ of its modeling. The old priest, also (Plate XLVIII*a*), which is of the eleventh century, is inimitable. Realism is rampant, both in the closely modeled head and hands, and in the minutely studied drapery, but note that this realism, unlike that of the present day, sacrificed nothing of the general to the particular; the statue is an eternal type, not an evanescent photograph, yet a portrait withal, intimate and intense.

In the Kamakura period, that is, the thirteenth century, all schools seem to meet and yet preserve their identity. We have the hieratic type represented in Plate XLVII*b* and in the supreme wonder of the Daibutsu; the school of force and action shown in the two Ni-o from Kofukuji (Plate XLIX); finally the school of portraiture, an example of which may be seen

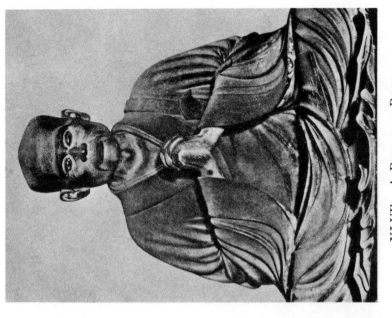

XLVIb A BUDDHIST PRIEST

XLVIa A PORTRAIT BUST

XLVIIb An Hieratic Figure

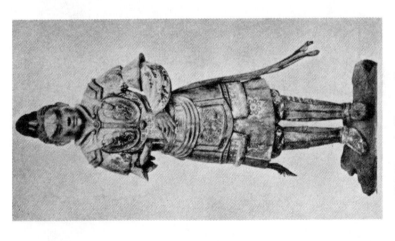

XLVIIa A Young Daimyo

XLVIIIa

XLVIIIb

Two Priestly Portraits

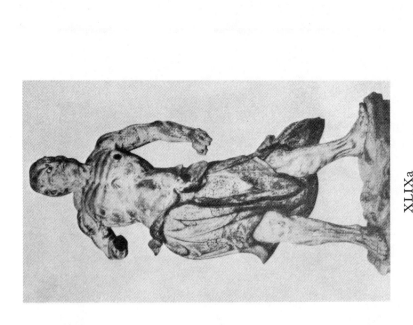

XLIXa

XLIXb

Two Ni-o from Kofukuji

in the study of a priest by Unkei (Plate XLVIII*b*).

This last is just as notable in its closeness to nature as the work of the Kyoto period, and higher praise cannot be given. I think the two Ni-o are simply the most marvelous examples of power, action, and life manifested without the smallest sacrifice of sculpturesque quality I have ever seen. Anatomically they are marvels and show a closeness of observation and a power of selection of significant details that are amazing. And what could be better than the sweep and rush of the drapery, what more perfectly rhythmic and decorative than the composition and drawing of the component folds; this is art, and art of the highest.

In a way, however, it is in the hieratic manifestations of religious faith, in such consummate triumphs as the great Buddha of Kamakura (see Frontispiece), that this period, if not all Japanese sculpture, reaches its culmination. Vast as the statue is, no less than fifty-two feet high, every detail except such as are absolutely necessary is eliminated, and the result is the triumphant apotheosis of the abstract and the universal. As one comes suddenly before this vision of brooding calm, shrined in the green calyx of the everlasting hills, the impression is almost overpowering. It is a lesson in the perfect adequacy of simple means to the greatest of all ends, a final proof that Japanese sculpture is a component part of the greatest sculpture of the world, a vindication of the claim that may be made for the nameless statuaries of Nippon to stand with those others, who in Europe wrought such masterpieces as the Victory of Samothrace, the St. George of Donatello, the King Arthur of Innsbruck, the St. Mary of Notre Dame.

Long before the Pisani began chiseling out the restoration of sculpture in Italy, back farther before the unknown artist wrought his wonder of Our Lady of Paris, farther still, even before, and centuries before, the first of all the waybreakers of sculpture in Europe, drew from his

innermost consciousness the beautiful beginnings of art so long forgotten it was really new,
the Japanese, trained by their Korean leaders
and driven by the vitalizing spirit of Buddhism
enlivening the embers of an immemorial ethnic
religion, were building of themselves a school
of sculpture from which no element of greatness
was lacking. Enough remains to make possible a
reconstruction of the whole wonderful period
from the founding of Horiuji, to the fall of
Kamakura, eight centuries of progressive greatness. A virgin field, clamorous for the student
and the constructive critic. May his advent be
no longer delayed.

THE FUTURE OF JAPANESE ART

WITH the close of the nineteenth century art as a vital thing, a racial attribute, came to its end in Japan. For thirteen hundred years it had been an essential part of a varied but unbroken civilization. All true art, all art, that is, which is more than sporadic and episodical, is a component part of the culture of a race. It cannot be created, it is doubtful even if it may be fostered, consciously at any rate. It is a sign of wholesome life, of the acceptance of high ideals, and of an honest effort, whether successful or not, at putting them into practice. It has never existed without religion of some sort as its supreme impulse and its ultimate goal.

The art of Japan, like the art of Hellenism and of Medieval Christianity, was the natural and inevitable expression of this plexus of conditions and tendencies. It was one of the first fruits of the Buddhist mission of the sixth century, and as that mission within two hundred years fixed a permanent type of lofty civilization in Japan, so did art follow step by step. For another thousand years this civilization continued through many vicissitudes, though never lapsing into, or even tending towards, barbarism. The art history was identical, the modes of its manifestation were various: now architecture, now painting, then literature, sculpture, the drama, or again the industrial arts. Note, however, that nothing intrinsically bad was ever done, all was good, better, or best.

The religious inspiration of Buddhism and the overmastering loyalty of Shinto fixed a type of character, chivalrous, honourable, self-sacrificing, that has persisted without visible weakening or failure until this day. The same impulses, or the racial character they created, established a standard of art and gave the power of production, that continued also without lapse or halting — not until this day, but until within the memory of men still young. Japanese character is one of the very great forces in contemporary world-civilization: Japanese art, the intimate and exact expression thereof, has ceased. The motive continues; the noble qualities that are clamorous for voicing are still extant, but their great artistic exponent is a thing of the past. The last great racial art has perished from the earth; the chapter is closed.

But is the chapter closed? So far as we can see, yes; inexorably: but if so it is a catastrophe comparable with the destruction of the Alexandrian libraries, the coming of the Goths and Vandals, the suppression of the English monasteries. From the beginning of the sixteenth century in Europe, art as a mode of civilization has been sinking lower and lower by successive stages, reaching about 1850 the lowest point recorded in history. Since then, while there have been fitful and sporadic instances of splendid recovery, they have been personal only, never racial (unless we except music amongst Teutonic peoples), and the communal nature of art, the only sense in which it is of profound importance, was farther from the possibility of restoration than ever before.

In Japan, however, communal art, the art which is the heritage of all the people, and is their highest mode of self-expression, had continued unmitigated and undefiled almost a century and a half after it had become extinct in Europe and America. Seventy-five years ago, when we were prostrate in unexampled artistic barbarism, Japan was still artistically intact: her civilization was therefore complete and well rounded and might still serve as the cherished flame for the rekindling of the dead fires of the West.

No one can say this now. In three centuries we have sold our birthright for a mess of pottage. Japan bartered hers in less than forty years.

Yet again, and because of the terrible significance of the fact, we must ask, is the chapter

closed forever? So far as we can see, yes: inexorably. Architecture has fallen into the hands of
tenth-rate German bunglers and their native
imitators, who copy so cleverly that their pro-
ductions are almost as bad as those of their
teachers. Painting is now running in European
lines; students devote themselves to studies
from the cast, the nude, and still life, ultimately
learning to turn out exceedingly clever imita-
tions in oil and water colours, which would be
creditable as exhibits in the Royal Academy and
the Salon. Sculpture is now purely imitative and
valuable from the standpoint of the forger. The
industrial arts are prostituted to the most pitiful
ends, and the cloisonné, lacquer, porcelain and
embroideries that now flood the auction rooms
of the West are valuable only in their dexterity,
and as showing how keenly and quickly a crafty
people can grasp and adapt itself to the demands
of artistic savagery. The loveliest landscape God
ever created is made horrible by rank on rank of
ghastly and insolent signs that would raise a

howl even in the Midland counties of England, and the bare reaches of Connecticut and New Jersey. " Marching through Georgia " has become a musical favourite with the people, our plays are being translated into Japanese, and the national costume, beautiful, economical, perfectly adapted to racial type and climatic conditions, is being discarded for trousers, dress skirts, picture hats, aniline coloured fabrics, and derbies.

Is the chapter closed? Yes, so far as we can see, inexorably. And yet a hope remains, for this extraordinary cataclysm has not carried with it the corresponding crash of ethical and spiritual standards. If we found the government of Japan honeycombed with venality and graft; if its industrial system had become an organized oligarchy of intimidation and spoliation; if the trust and corporation were supreme and implacable, yet accepted by the public with a grin half of envious admiration, half of careless indifference; if the sanctity of domestic life had crumbled away in corruption; if unearthly superstitions were doing duty as religious convictions and each was finding hordes of dupes, ready for the bleeding; if war brought protests from high finance and vested interests because their pockets were touched by the blow in self-defence, whilst the ranks of the armies could only be filled by conscription and refilled on account of desertions — if these were the accompaniments of the death of art, then indeed we might say with truth, the chapter is closed.

These things we have not found, nor any one of them,[1] therefore we are permitted to hope; for the extinction of art in Japan is the result of other causes than the collapse of racial character. There is no canker that has eaten the heart out of Japanese civilization, making art no longer a possibility: it is just as sound and wholesome and honourable and true as it was a century ago. If art is a result, not a product, then the generative conditions are just as vital as they

[1] But is this strictly true in this year 1930?

were under the Ashikaga or Tokugawa Shoguns. For once art may occur again as the result of conscious volition; the question is, will it have the chance, may we expect this as one of the fruits of victory?

It is possible: more than this, of course, no one can say, but Japanese character, as it is discovering itself to us, makes the thing conceivable.

When the ports were opened a curious situation developed: two civilizations confronted each other, of equal antiquity, yet utterly diverse. To the East the West was barbarism, and vice versa. The latter was contemporary, therefore immeasurably the stronger. The former was perfectly conscious of its own superiority in many things, but it found itself absolutely unable to meet its giant tyrant on anything approaching equal terms. The languages were different, therefore the weaker, the cloistered recluse, set himself to master the tongue of the powerful spoiler. Since the day of the — by courtesy

called — " Battle " of Shimonoseki, one object
has been before the Japanese as the goal of
every thought and every act: to meet the West
on its own field and win recognition for themselves as one of the Great Peoples and one of
the Great Powers.

Pride, national self-respect, is the heritage of
every Japanese: this people was determined to
prove its equality with any people of the West.
It has achieved its object in less than half a century, and by so doing written in history one of
the most amazing and romantic records of all
time. The method adopted was far different to
that in vogue in the West. No effort was made
to crush the fact down the throats of the scoffers:
this would have resulted simply in extinction.
Instead, and the story is too well known to need
detailed repetition, Japan quietly assimilated
every quality of the West, except its religion and
its political corruption; no task was too great;
first failure only meant second attempt and victory. One by one all the methods, and some of

the manners, of nineteenth-century Europe and America were taken over, assimilated, and made a part of what may be called exoteric Japan.

Everything but the fundamental principles of the race was discarded, and even those were sometimes masked and hidden away. Finally the monstrous treaties were revised and the first victory was won. The war with China promised a second victory, recognition as an equal, the end and aim of it all, but, at the very moment of final achievement, three nations leagued themselves in a shameful bond, not only to rob the victor of the signs of victory — that were a small matter — but to humiliate a triumphant nation and deny to her once more admission amongst those who thus proved, not that Japan was their inferior, but that she was what she had never claimed, immeasurably their superior.

The fact was clear to all but Russia, Germany, and France, but sentimental recognition was not enough, so Japan set her teeth and went to work again. For ten years she prepared to

fight Russia, just that and nothing more. We
knew this in Japan long years ago, but in the
West no one really thought this supposedly " little country " could dare such a thing. Well, the
truth is sufficiently evident now, and if defeat
should happen to follow again, unless the race
were utterly exterminated preparations would
continue for twenty years, or a century. In the
end one result only is possible.

The great contest may end in final victory
today or tomorrow. If so, if Japan at last steps
forward, one of the great civilized Powers of the
earth, recognized as such by all the world, what
will be the result? Many things in which no man
could avow his faith and escape the stigma of
insanity; but there is one that may develop and
this may be said fearlessly, and that is the absolute sloughing off of the absurd habiliments of
Western and Westernized art, and the rebirth
of the art of Japan in all its original splendour.

As I have said above, if the outward trans-
formation of Japan had involved the destruction

of character, the loss of ideals, this could not be said, but Japanese character is intact. It has been overlaid by many thicknesses of strange vesture, but these may prove only defensive armour, protecting the wearer from the blows of a novel and unfamiliar assailant. Commercial trickery, political liberalism, free thought and atheism, these are evils that exist, and there are many others; but it is well within the range of possibility that all may prove merely temporary expedients, since they are not natural evolutions from the psychological history of the people, but have been assumed arbitrarily, and, unless they have instilled a fatal virus into the social organism, an assumption for which there is no justification in fact thus far, may be as arbitrarily cast aside.

The politician who argues of " natural rights," the slender aristocrat who wears tan shoes and a derby hat, the shop-keeper who cheats one smilingly and with exquisite taste, the geisha who demands champagne rather than sake, the

L   A Vision of Fujiyama

peasant woman who clothes her child in a knitted woolen jacket made in America and dyed a poisonous magenta with aniline dyes, the soshi who spits contemptuously as you pass by — all these are of one ilk, they are all varied manifestations of a national movement for national recognition. They may go no deeper than this: to those who know the first rudiments of Japanese character — and few can know more — it is perfectly conceivable that every itemized Westernizer in the nation is secretly scornful of the things he outwardly glories in, and laughing meanwhile within himself at the credulity of the innocent foreigners who do not see that it is all no more than a rather unsavoury, but also indispensable, means to an end.

Japan has borrowed much from the West that she will never throw away, but these are the solid materialities: steam and electricity and industrial machinery; medicine, surgery, sanitary systems; the organization, maintenance, and utilization of an army and navy. Civilization of a noble type is still possible with these, and Japan has made them her own, establishing her title through a better use of them thus far than was made by those who brought them into being.

But the waste and slag and refuse of scientific and industrial civilization, the noxious emanations of our great seething ferment of life, these are of no use to Japan when her victory is won, and these — the hope shines out again — may go.

We have destroyed three-fourths of the valuable things of life through misusing the mighty engines we have fashioned, now these marvelous creations fall into new hands: is it madness to believe that in Japan may be solved the problems of making science and industrialism minister to the noblest ideals, not to the meanest; create beauty of thought and life and conduct instead of working against it?

I believe that the morrow of victory will show the beginning of a new dispensation. Nothing of Westernism that is fundamentally good

will be discarded, but instead there may be a
swift and startling recrudescence of nation-
ality, of " Yamato Damashii," testing every new
thing, not by the measure of opportunism, but
by the standards of sound, religious, and beautiful culture. Japan is effectually disguised, but
Japan is there, underneath, and in due time the
disguise may be thrown off. When this day
comes, there will occur certain changes that will
be very shocking to our sensibilities, for a time
at least. Many of them will be radical and super-
ficially reactionary; they will appear in the laws
and the Fundamental Law, in education, in commerce, in manufacture. Japan will say to the
Powers of the West, " Gentlemen, I thank you;
you have forged for me the weapons with which
I have justified my claim to be considered a
great, civilized Power. In many ways, however,
I consider my own civilization as superior to
yours, and I shall now revert to these better
ways, after an experience which, if not aways
savoury, has been invariably instructive. Though

I have already paid your price (a heavy one) for all you have sold me, I have no grounds for complaint, and you are heartily welcome to learn of me as I have learned of you. Particularly shall I be glad to demonstrate to you that liberty necessarily destroys neither manners nor laws; that the whole is greater than the part, and that chivalry and self-sacrifice are the foundations of the State as well as of society; that beauty, whether of act, or custom, or costume, or handiwork, is a means of discriminating between a civilized man and a barbarian. Finally, I shall be glad to show you that knowledge does not destroy faith."

Is the chapter closed? Yes, but not, perhaps, inexorably. We are dealing with a non-Aryan race, with a type of mind of which we know almost nothing, with a civilization untouched by any of the influences that have molded our own; anything is possible. At the same time there exist certain fundamental qualities which mark the whole human race, while into the considera-

tion comes an immemorial ancestor worship, reverence for the dead and pride in racial achievements that must influence very radically every
action of the Japanese people. For those reasons,
I believe that racial instinct and moral conviction will result in a sudden and amazing return
to all that was good in the old Japan, including,
of course, its art. There are signs of this even
now. The laws compelling the assumption of
European dress on certain occasions have been
greatly relaxed. The many followers of Professor Okakura are fighting for the conservation
of national ideals in painting. There is a visible
revolt against the shocking architecture that in
the name of Europeanism has defiled the land:
in spite of occasional absurdities of fashion the
drama and music are still comparatively sound.
A word from the right source, the one supreme
source, the Mikado, would send the whole ridicu-
lous card house of Western art and Western
manners crumbling into instantaneous collapse.
Will the word be spoken? I firmly believe so, for

the Emperor Mutsuhito has shown himself always, not only a wise sovereign, but the very incarnation of the spirit of Japan.[1] He knows even better than we of the West how infinitely his country and his people will gain by a dignified and self-respecting resumption of much that for the time has been cast away. Such a course would fix Japanese civilization as an indestructible entity for another period, and world civilization would gain thereby. Finally, it would command the respect and frank admiration of the West, and no one could say again, " The Japanese are clever, but only as imitators."

When the hour is ripe, I believe the word will be spoken.

[1] This essay was written in the year 1895.

CONCLUSION

In writing a postscript for the new edition of
this book I find myself at a disadvantage in that
I have not revisited Japan since the impressions
here recorded were registered so many years ago.
I have no first-hand knowledge of what has happened in architecture and the allied arts; on the
other hand the developments, particularly in
architecture, have been given wide publicity and
here one may judge of results, perhaps even of
tendencies, without personal contact. Of possible
mutations in racial character, of developments in
political and social institutions, it is impossible
to speak, since the only evidence is what happens
to be recorded in the annals of international
councils and conferences or in newspaper reports
of current events, neither of which is a safe basis

of judgment when it comes to fundamental things. Here then silence alone is becoming.

As I already have said, these impressions were gathered just after the war with China and during the Spanish-American War. Most of the papers were written during the contest between Russia and Japan with the resulting victorious war. All these events directly or indirectly influenced the Westernizing process of transforming an isolated, aristocratic, Oriental nation into an Occidental, industrialized, progressive community with corresponding reactions in all branches of art. Twenty-five years ago only a madman or a seer would have predicated the World War as the event that would arrive to crown this long process of Westernization that began with the opening of the ports by Commodore Perry and culminated in a world-cataclysm that suddenly raised Japan to a position where she was a co-equal ally with one group of Great Powers in their conflict with another group of equal status, and left her at last the peer in world affairs of

Great Britain, France, Italy and the United States.

The goal of national endeavour has at last been reached. Whether this is for good or ill only the future can prove, but the answer can hardly be delayed more than another twenty-five years. If the West is destined to fall of the weight of its own industrialization and the folly of its distorted democracy then Japan also falls and Commodore Perry will be recorded in future histories not as the emancipator of Japan but as her nemesis. If the West weathers the test now in process and issues into a new era of more lofty ideals, saner methods and a juster standard of values, then Japan may find herself in a position of leadership, not only amongst the nations of the West but in that East of which she is, at least geographically, a part and that is now in ferment and revolt with anarchy only a little distance away.

There is food for thought in the fact that this seething ferment that extends from the Western frontiers of Soviet Russia to the eastern shores of the Sea of Japan and from the Arctic Ocean to the Soudan, Ceylon and the Philippine Islands, is the direct result of these two forces that now control, and so controlling threaten the whole future of Europe and America with final disaster; that is to say, industrial, commercial and technological civilization and that distorted and deliquescent political and social democracy that already in so large a part of Europe has forced the return of an old tyranny through absolute dictatorships as the only escape from its futilities and its parlous misadventures. Dimly and gropingly forecasting something of this when these essays were first written, I had in mind the persistence, vital and intact, of the Japanese soul, however overlaid this might be with the opportunist vesture of an assumed and expedient Westernism, and its emergence, at the time of crisis, for the salvaging and redemption of a world gone wrong. I did, indeed, envisage an ultimate sloughing off of this assumed garb of expediency, once the goal of world-recognition had been attained. Well, the

LIa

LIb

TWO EXAMPLES OF EUROPEAN ARCHITECTURE, TOKYO

event is now an accomplished fact, but is there any sign of this resurgence of " Yamato Damashii " ? Not that as yet the eye can perceive. So far as one can judge the ignis fatuus of technological culture and industrial-commercial supremacy is still the guiding light of contemporary Japan. It may be that it is too soon after the consummation of a racial and national hope to expect such revelation. After all it is hardly more than a matter of a decade. Also the civilization of the West is still triumphant, weakening only here and there along the edges, with the threat of dissolution still vague and uncertain. It may be that this spirit of an old culture that lasted in Japan so much longer than elsewhere is only the immutable call: " come over and help us."

In the meantime it is quite clear that architecturally there is no sign, so far as the indigenous product is concerned, of anything except Westernism of the most pronounced type, declining even on " modernism." It is curious that the earthquake and fire that wiped out Tokyo and Yokohama gave just the abnormal opportunity for an excessive amount of new building that happened in the case of the great fire of London in the time of Charles II. There Christopher Wren, an engineer of defective ability with a flare for architecture of the theoretical sort, seized his first opportunity and made a great show of the Palladian Renaissance that otherwise might have remained a rather secondary manifestation of an alien art. Here, in Tokyo, the ground being so almost wholly swept clean, there was an equal, even a greater opportunity. Technological and industrial civilization being then firmly in the saddle, and the old culture quite completely " filed for reference " the new city was inevitably of the highly modern ilk. Judging from the photographs, it is a replica of a prosperous and ambitious city of the Middle West with, as the directing force behind it, a rather unusually high standard of architectural achievement. I should not like to see Tokyo now for the two Americas furnish a sufficiency of this sort of thing and do it quite well enough.

After all, though, given the great distinction and the dominance of a new economic and social system, what else could logically have been done? One can hardly visualize Standard Oil offices raised on the lines of Kumamoto Castle, or a department store or garage or moving picture palace aping Byodo-in in steel and concrete. Probably the same is true in the case of a palace for the housing of Parliament with its full compliment of political parties and blocs, responsible ministries and legislative committees, log-rolling " pork barrels " and multitudinous unnecessary laws, and all the other rather futile paraphernalia of representative government. We in the United States smile at our one " Gothic " state capitol, even at the Medieval Miracle of Parliament Houses in London, recognizing their impropriety, while conversely we bow in admiration before so modern a creation as the Nebraska Capitol. The new thing cannot be housed in recreated forms out of the past, no matter how well they may be fashioned, and the civilization of today, whether it flourishes in Europe or America or Japan is a new thing with only the most tenuous linkage with the past, if any, and so it must build for itself, if not " more stately mansions " at least those that are more logical and consistent.

So Japan is undoubtedly right in remaking Tokyo in the most approved Western lines, particularly since she does it so well. The old Yedo is gone, and the old Nippon. A new metropolis and a new world state have taken their places. The choice has been made and deliberately. How far does the change go, how deep beneath the surface? Kyoto and Nara remain substantially, I believe, unchanged, while Tokyo and Yokohama and Nagasaki go on their chosen way. Are the old cities in their grave changelessness a symbol of what still may be " resting quietly under the drums and tramplings " of industrial conquest, awaiting the day when the new

LIII THE DREAM OF A PARLIAMENT HOUSE

LII   TEIKOKU HOTEL, TOKYO

shall pass even as the old, and the old return once more refreshed and revivified? It
may be.

If in architecture Japan is playing a logical and
consistent part in her policy of systematic Westernization, I cannot find the same excuse for her
painters and sculptors, at least for some of them;
those that deliberately forsake the unique tradition of their own ethnicate. Architecture does
and must express concrete things. True, in all its
higher reaches it expresses also spiritual intangi-
bles, but all operating energies must be housed,
from the cathedral and the university to the
stock exchange and the cinema, the department
store, the railway station and the chamber of
commerce. These must show what they are,
through the forms that are created to give them
logical expression. With painting, sculpture, music, the case is, I conceive, quite different. These
arts deal with spiritual values and with the eternal struggle of man to apprehend them. These
values may be mystical, amorphous, transcen-

dental, or they may be values of that beauty that is apprehended through the senses: colour, form entities, musical sounds in mysterious but plangent and evocative combination. They are not material in any sense, nor are they subject to change through altered economic and social and political conditions. The plastic art of Egypt, Greece, the Middle Ages, the early Renaissance, old China, old Japan, is essentially one art, however sundered may be these epochs, however diverse their racial streams, however varied their forms and their technical methods. Good art always represents the *best* in any time, amongst any people, and usually this " best " reveals itself not in the avowed theories and principles of a people, or in its institutions, but only through its art.

Why then must there be this turning away on the part of so many Japanese artists from the art that was so consistent, so representative and so supreme? And why must they think they must study in the West and copy the alien art of the

West? If we ourselves were sure of what we wanted or how to do it, there might be more superficial justification for such a course, but as a matter of fact we are not consciously apprised of either. During the last fifty years we have had almost as many vogues — fashions you could hardly call them — in painting and only a lesser number in sculpture, poetry and music. Of late one has been about as irrational and uncouth as the other, while anything approaching consistency or a logical progression of development has been completely lacking. It may be that this vagrant " art " adequately expresses the dominant factors in current civilization, but it would be rude to say so, and let us hope, at least an exaggeration. Yet it is just this rather helpless wandering that has become the pattern for many Japanese, and it seems a pity. Certainly it can lead nowhere in spite of the fact that our disciples do the thing admirably; but why do it? In no respect does it represent the underlying and essential spirit of Japan; it does not in the least increase Western respect and it can scarcely give pleasure.

One can understand in a way the overproduction of " export work " for a demand will invariably create a supply, no matter how unjustifiable it may be. If the West wants inferior " arts and crafts " — and it certainly does — it will find the shops full and the dealers receptive. Painting and sculpture, however, are a different matter. There is no demand for any form of æsthetic modernism or realism as interpreted by Japanese artists, so the commercial excuse is nonexistent. What other reason there may be passes comprehension.

Of course, this, so to speak, artistic movement is by no means universal. There still are, I believe, consistent Japanese who refuse to have any part in this betrayal of national and racial ideals. Men who hold to the established ways in painting and sculpture and even in architecture, though I fear the latter at least must be practising their art as a matter of principle, not as a source of revenue. It is a curious fact that in this art at least it is foreigners who chiefly ask for some continuance of the ancient style and foreign architects who try in their ardent but blundering way to reproduce it. It is true both for Japan and China that much of the school and hospital building that is controlled by American agencies does try to make some approximation to racial architecture and recently I have seen a Christian church and its subsidiary buildings designed and erected after a fashion most cleverly adapted from the models of Tokugawa Buddhist architecture. It would be a singular turn of fate if that very West that forced Japan into the modern world and made her subject to Westernism in its most exaggerated form, should be the agency which preserved the old ways of national art for a new day.

Somehow these old ways must be preserved, not alone for the art of Japan but for what underlies it and gives it force, makes it possible in fact, and that is a real standard of values, and the

sane, happy and beautiful life that follows there-
from. It is hardly conceivable that the new life
and the new philosophy of life that, following on
with the rest of the world, Japan has chosen,
should be in effect better than the old. If this
were true it would rather destroy one's confidence in man as an institution (assuming that
that confidence still measurably endures) and
would quite take the meaning out of life. It
would be like saying that the Hyksos period in
Egypt was better than the IVth Dynasty, the
Dark Ages of Western Europe than the Hellenic
Era, the eighteenth century than the thirteenth.

No, what is happening now, both in the East
and in the West, is not an epoch but an episode;
not a progression but a retrogression in their nature, and happening with an almost stolid regu-
larity always prepare the way for another advance, and this we can count on with perfect
confidence. When the preparation is accomplished " offences must come " but if it is " woe
to him by whom the offence cometh " it is equally

sure that in the end there is all honour to him who, with quiet composure and in isolation, keeps alight the little flame through great darkness for the lighting of an ultimate future. Such was the work of the monks of the Dark Ages, and great was the conflagration they kindled once the Middle Ages came to power. There are many in the world today who treasure the heritage of a great past — Classical, Medieval, Renaissance — confident that the time will come when its value will be seen again, its potency recognized, its operation initiated anew. With these must be counted those who in Japan still hoard the treasure of antiquity, not in the arts alone but in all that makes for righteousness and beauty and joy in life; in a word, Yamato Damashii.

INDEX

A

Absolute beauty, Eastern solution of mystery of, 171; first requisite of art, 173.

Architectural styles, sequence of East and West, 89.

Architecture of Japan, misjudged, 34; example of perfect development, 37; one of great styles of the world, 38; Sino-Korean style of, 40; classical traces in, 45; destruction of early, 48; becomes merged in decoration, 61; curve composition in, 63; modern domestic, 70, 121; modern domestic, debasement of, 71; critical estimate of, 73; lessons to be learned from, 74; proportion in, 74; simplicity in domestic, 76; use of natural woods in, 77; sense of proportion in domestic, 77; classical traces in, 87; spiritual import in, 90; primitive Shinto, 92; destruction of early, 96; perfect style in wood, 123, 124.

Art of Japan, fundamentally one with that of Europe, 28; based on communism of her civilization, 31; greatest when most conservative, 31; standards established by, 32;

Western discovery of, 148; last to be extinguished, 149; and that of Europe in the eighth century, 150; and that of Europe in the sixteenth century, 149; primarily Chinese, 153; four periods of, 157; fostering conditions of, 160; carelessness a crime in, 162; ugliness a sin in, 162; ludicrous nineteenth century estimate of, 165; lesson of, 167; technical perfection of, 174; selection, emphasis and idealization in, 185.

Art, the fall of Japanese, 209.

"Arts and Crafts in Japan," 156.

Ashikaga, fall of the, 59.

Ashikaga period, 55; architectural style of, 101; artistic supremacy of, 155; great artists of, 155.

B

Bathrooms and baths, 133.

Buddhism, incentive power of, towards art, 161.

Buddhist civilization, downfall of, 107.

C

Castle architecture, 65.

Castle-keeps, construction of, 70.

Dover Books on Art

Dover Books on Art

THE FOUR BOOKS OF ARCHITECTURE, Andrea Palladio. A compendium of the art of Andrea Palladio, one of the most celebrated architects of the Renaissance, including 250 magnificently-engraved plates showing edifices either of Palladio's design or reconstructed (in these drawings) by him from classical ruins and contemporary accounts. 257 plates. xxiv + 119pp. 9½ x 12¾. T1308 Clothbound $10.00

150 MASTERPIECES OF DRAWING, A. Toney. Selected by a gifted artist and teacher, these are some of the finest drawings produced by Western artists from the early 15th to the end of the 18th centuries. Excellent reproductions of drawings by Rembrandt, Bruegel, Raphael, Watteau, and other familiar masters, as well as works by lesser known but brilliant artists. 150 plates. xviii + 150pp. 5⅜ x 11¼. T1032 Paperbound $2.00

MORE DRAWINGS BY HEINRICH KLEY. Another collection of the graphic, vivid sketches of Heinrich Kley, one of the most diabolically talented cartoonists of our century. The sketches take in every aspect of human life: nothing is too sacred for him to ridicule, no one too eminent for him to satirize. 158 drawings you will not easily forget. iv + 104pp. 7⅜ x 10¾. T41 Paperbound $1.85

THE TRIUMPH OF MAXIMILIAN I, 137 Woodcuts by Hans Burgkmair and Others. This is one of the world's great art monuments, a series of magnificent woodcuts executed by the most important artists in the German realms as part of an elaborate plan by Maximilian I, ruler of the Holy Roman Empire, to commemorate his own name, dynasty, and achievements. 137 plates. New translation of descriptive text, notes, and bibliography prepared by Stanley Appelbaum. Special section of 10pp. containing a reduced version of the entire Triumph. x + 169pp. 11⅛ x 9¼. T1207 Paperbound $3.00

LOST EXAMPLES OF COLONIAL ARCHITECTURE, J. M. Howells. This book offers a unique guided tour through America's architectural past, all of which is either no longer in existence or so changed that its original beauty has been destroyed. More than 275 clear photos of old churches, dwelling houses, public buildings, business structures, etc. 245 plates, containing 281 photos and 9 drawings, floorplans, etc. New Index. xvii + 248pp. 7⅞ x 10¾. T1143 Paperbound $2.75

Dover Books on Art

200 DECORATIVE TITLE-PAGES, edited by A. Nesbitt. Fascinating and informative from a historical point of view, this beautiful collection of decorated titles will be a great inspiration to students of design, commercial artists, advertising designers, etc. A complete survey of the genre from the first known decorated title to work in the first decades of this century. Bibliography and sources of the plates. 222pp. 8⅜ x 11¼.

T1264 Paperbound $2.75

ON THE LAWS OF JAPANESE PAINTING, H. P. Bowie. This classic work on the philosophy and technique of Japanese art is based on the author's first-hand experiences studying art in Japan. Every aspect of Japanese painting is described: the use of the brush and other materials; laws governing conception and execution; subjects for Japanese paintings, etc. The best possible substitute for a series of lessons from a great Oriental master. Index. xv + 117pp. + 66 plates. 6⅛ x 9¼.

T30 Paperbound $2.00

PAINTING IN THE FAR EAST, L. Binyon. A study of over 1500 years of Oriental art by one of the world's outstanding authorities. The author chooses the most important masters in each period—Wu Tao-tzu, Toba Sojo, Kanaoka, Li Lung-mien, Masanobu, Okio, etc.—and examines the works, schools, and influence of each within their cultural context. 42 photographs. Sources of original works and selected bibliography. Notes including list of principal painters by periods. xx + 297pp. 6⅛ x 9¼.

T520 Paperbound $2.25

THE ALPHABET AND ELEMENTS OF LETTERING, F. W. Goudy. A beautifully illustrated volume on the aesthetics of letters and type faces and their history and development. Each plate consists of 15 forms of a single letter with the last plate devoted to the ampersand and the numerals. "A sound guide for all persons engaged in printing or drawing," Saturday Review. 27 full-page plates. 48 additional figures. xii + 131pp. 7⅞ x 10¾.

T792 Paperbound $2.00

PAINTING IN ISLAM, Sir Thomas W. Arnold. This scholarly study puts Islamic painting in its social and religious context and examines its relation to Islamic civilization in general. 65 full-page plates illustrate the text and give outstanding examples of Islamic art. 4 appendices. Index of mss. referred to. General Index. xxiv + 159pp. 6⅝ x 9¼. T1310 Paperbound $2.50

Dover Books on Art

THE HISTORY AND TECHNIQUE OF LETTERING, A. Nesbitt. A thorough history of lettering from the ancient Egyptians to the present, and a 65-page course in lettering for artists. Every major development in lettering history is illustrated by a complete aphabet. Fully analyzes such masters as Caslon, Koch, Garamont, Jenson, and many more. 89 alphabets, 165 other specimens. 317pp. 7½ x 10½.   T427 Paperbound $2.00

LETTERING AND ALPHABETS, J. A. Cavanagh. An unabridged reissue of "Lettering," containing the full discussion, analysis, illustration of 89 basic hand lettering styles based on Caslon, Bodoni, Gothic, many other types. Hundreds of technical hints on construction, strokes, pens, brushes, etc. 89 alphabets, 72 lettered specimens, which may be reproduced permission-free. 121pp. 9¾ x 8.   T53 Paperbound $1.35

THE HUMAN FIGURE IN MOTION, Eadweard Muybridge. The largest collection in print of Muybridge's famous high-speed action photos. 4789 photographs in more than 500 action-strip-sequences (at shutter speeds up to 1/6000th of a second) illustrate men, women, children—mostly undraped—performing such actions as walking, running, getting up, lying down, carrying objects, throwing, etc. "An unparalleled dictionary of action for all artists," AMERICAN ARTIST. 390 full-page plates, with 4789 photographs. Heavy glossy stock, reinforced binding with headbands. 7⅞ x 10¾.   T204 Clothbound $10.00

ANIMALS IN MOTION, Eadweard Muybridge. The largest collection of animal action photos in print. 34 different animals (horses, mules, oxen, goats, camels, pigs, cats, lions, gnus, deer, monkeys, eagles—and 22 others) in 132 characteristic actions. All 3919 photographs are taken in series at speeds up to 1/1600th of a second, offering artists, biologists, cartoonists a remarkable opportunity to see exactly how an ostrich's head bobs when running, how a lion puts his foot down, how an elephant's knee bends, how a bird flaps his wings, thousands of other hard-to-catch details. "A really marvellous series of plates," NATURE. 380 full-page plates. Heavy glossy stock, reinforced binding with headbands. 7⅞ x 10¾.   T203 Clothbound $10.00

BASIC BOOKBINDING, A. W. Lewis. Enables both beginners and experts to rebind old books or bind paperbacks in hard covers. Treats materials, tools; gives step-by-step instruction in how to collate a book, sew it, back it, make boards, etc. 261 illus. Appendices. 155pp. 5⅜ x 8.   T169 Paperbound $1.45

Dover Books on Art

PRINCIPLES OF ART HISTORY, H. Wölfflin. This remarkably instructive work demonstrates the tremendous change in artistic conception from the 14th to the 18th centuries, by analyzing 164 works by Botticelli, Dürer, Hobbema, Holbein, Hals, Titian, Rembrandt, Vermeer, etc., and pointing out exactly what is meant by "baroque," "classic," "primitive," "picturesque," and other basic terms of art history and criticism. "A remarkable lesson in the art of seeing," SAT. REV. OF LITERATURE. Translated from the 7th German edition. 150 illus. 254pp. 6⅛ x 9¼. **T276 Paperbound $2.00**

FOUNDATIONS OF MODERN ART, A. Ozenfant. Stimulating discussion of human creativity from paleolithic cave painting to modern painting, architecture, decorative arts. Fully illustrated with works of Gris, Lipchitz, Léger, Picasso, primitive, modern artifacts, architecture, industrial art, much more. 226 illustrations. 368pp. 6⅛ x 9¼. **T215 Paperbound $2.25**

METALWORK AND ENAMELLING, H. Maryon. Probably the best book ever written on the subject. Tells everything necessary for the home manufacture of jewelry, rings, ear pendants, bowls, etc. Covers materials, tools, soldering, filigree, setting stones, raising patterns, repoussé work, damascening, niello, cloisonné, polishing, assaying, casting, and dozens of other techniques. The best substitute for apprenticeship to a master metalworker. 363 photos and figures. 374pp. 5½ x 8½. **T183 Clothbound $8.50**

SHAKER FURNITURE, E. D. and F. Andrews. The most illuminating study of Shaker furniture ever written. Covers chronology, craftsmanship, houses, shops, etc. Includes over 200 photographs of chairs, tables, clocks, beds, benches, etc. "Mr. & Mrs. Andrews know all there is to know about Shaker furniture," Mark Van Doren, NATION. 48 full-page plates. 192pp. 7⅞ x 10¾. **T679 Paperbound $2.00**

ANIMAL DRAWING: ANATOMY AND ACTION FOR ARTISTS, C. R. Knight. 158 studies, with full accompanying text, of such animals as the gorilla, bear, bison, dromedary, camel, vulture, pelican, iguana, shark, etc., by one of the greatest modern masters of animal drawing. Innumerable tips on how to get life expression into your work. "An excellent reference work," SAN FRANCISCO CHRONICLE. 158 illustrations. 156pp. 10½ x 8½. **T426 Paperbound $2.00**

Dover Books on Art

AFRICAN SCULPTURE, Ladislas Segy. 163 full-page plates illustrating masks, fertility figures, ceremonial objects, etc., of 50 West and Central African tribes—95% never before illustrated. 34-page introduction to African sculpture. "Mr. Segy is one of its top authorities," NEW YORKER. 164 full-page photographic plates. Introduction. Bibliography. 244pp. 6⅛ x 9¼.

T396 Paperbound $2.00

CALLIGRAPHY, J. G. Schwandner. First reprinting in 200 years of this legendary book of beautiful handwriting. Over 300 ornamental initials, 12 complete calligraphic alphabets, over 150 ornate frames and panels, 75 calligraphic pictures of cherubs, stags, lions, etc., thousands of flourishes, scrolls, etc., by the greatest 18th-century masters. All material can be copied or adapted without permission. Historical introduction. 158 full-page plates. 368pp. 9 x 13.

T475 Clothbound $10.00

A DIDEROT PICTORIAL ENCYCLOPEDIA OF TRADES AND INDUSTRY. Manufacturing and the Technical Arts in Plates Selected from "L'Encyclopédie ou Dictionnaire Raisonné des Sciences, des Arts, et des Métiers," of Denis Diderot, edited with text by C. Gillispie. Over 2000 illustrations on 485 full-page plates. Magnificent 18th-century engravings of men, women, and children working at such trades as milling flour, cheesemaking, charcoal burning, mining, silverplating, shoeing horses, making fine glass, printing, hundreds more, showing details of machinery, different steps in sequence, etc. A remarkable art work, but also the largest collection of working figures in print, copyright-free, for art directors, designers, etc. Two vols. 920pp. 9 x 12. Heavy library cloth.

T421 Two volume set $18.50

SILK SCREEN TECHNIQUES, J. Biegeleisen, M. Cohn. A practical step-by-step home course in one of the most versatile, least expensive graphic arts processes. How to build an inexpensive silk screen, prepare stencils, print, achieve special textures, use color, etc. Every step explained, diagrammed. 149 illustrations, 201pp. 6⅛ x 9¼.

T433 Paperbound $1.75

STICKS AND STONES, Lewis Mumford. An examination of forces influencing American architecture: the medieval tradition in early New England, the classical influence in Jefferson's time, the Brown Decades, the imperial facade, the machine age, etc. "A truly remarkable book," SAT. REV. OF LITERATURE. 2nd revised edition. 21 illus. xvii + 240pp. 5⅜ x 8.

T202 Paperbound $1.75

Dover Books on Art

LANDSCAPE GARDENING IN JAPAN, Josiah Conder. A detailed picture of Japanese gardening techniques and ideas, the artistic principles incorporated in the Japanese garden, and the religious and ethical concepts at the heart of those principles. Preface. 92 illustrations, plus all 40 full-page plates from the Supplement. Index. xv + 299pp. 8⅜ x 11¼.
T1216 Paperbound $2.75

DESIGN AND FIGURE CARVING, E. J. Tangerman. "Anyone who can peel a potato can carve," states the author, and in this unusual book he shows you how, covering every stage in detail from very simple exercises working up to museum-quality pieces. Terrific aid for hobbyists, arts and crafts counselors, teachers, those who wish to make reproductions for the commercial market. Appendix: How to Enlarge a Design. Brief bibliography. Index. 1298 figures. x + 289pp. 5⅜ x 8½.
T1209 Paperbound $1.85

WILD FOWL DECOYS, Joel Barber. Antique dealers, collectors, craftsmen, hunters, readers of Americana, etc. will find this the only thorough and reliable guide on the market today to this unique folk art. It contains the history, cultural significance, regional design variations; unusual decoy lore; working plans for constructing decoys; and loads of illustrations. 140 full-page plates, 4 in color. 14 additional plates of drawings and plans by the author. xxvii + 156pp. 7⅞ x 10¾.   T11 Paperbound $2.75

1800 WOODCUTS BY THOMAS BEWICK AND HIS SCHOOL. This is the largest collection of first-rate pictorial woodcuts in print—an indispensable part of the working library of every commercial artist, art director, production designer, packaging artist, craftsman, manufacturer, librarian, art collector, and artist. And best of all, when you buy your copy of Bewick, you buy the rights to reproduce individual illustrations—no permission needed, no acknowledgments, no clearance fees! Classified index. Bibliography and sources. xiv + 246pp. 9 x 12.
T766 Clothbound $10.00

THE SCRIPT LETTER, Tommy Thompson. Prepared by a noted authority, this is a thorough, straightforward course of instruction with advice on virtually every facet of the art of script lettering. Also a brief history of lettering with examples from early copy books and illustrations from present day advertising and packaging. Copiously illustrated. Bibliography. 128pp. 6½ x 9⅛.
T1311 Paperbound $1.00

Dover Books on Art

THE BOOK OF SIGNS, R. Koch. 493 symbols—crosses, monograms, astrological, biological symbols, runes, etc.—from ancient manuscripts, cathedrals, coins, catacombs, pottery. May be reproduced permission-free. 493 illustrations by Fritz Kredel. 104pp. 6⅛ x 9¼.　　　　　T162 Paperbound $1.00

A HANDBOOK OF EARLY ADVERTISING ART, C. P. Hornung. The largest collection of copyright-free early advertising art ever compiled. Vol. I: 2,000 illustrations of animals, old automobiles, buildings, allegorical figures, fire engines, Indians, ships, trains, more than 33 other categories! Vol. II: Over 4,000 typographical specimens; 600 Roman, Gothic, Barnum, Old English faces; 630 ornamental type faces; hundreds of scrolls, initials, flourishes, etc. "A remarkable collection," PRINTERS' INK.

Vol. I: Pictorial Volume. Over 2000 illustrations. 256pp. 9 x 12.
T122 Clothbound $10.00

Vol. II: Typographical Volume. Over 4000 specimens. 319pp. 9 x 12.　　　　　T123 Clothbound $10.00

Two volume set, Clothbound, only $18.50

THE AUTOBIOGRAPHY OF AN IDEA, Louis Sullivan. The architect whom Frank Lloyd Wright called "the master," records the development of the theories that revolutionized America's skyline. 34 full-page plates of Sullivan's finest work. New introduction by R. M. Line. xiv + 335pp. 5⅜ x 8.

T281 Paperbound $2.00

THE MATERIALS AND TECHNIQUES OF MEDIEVAL PAINTING, D. V. Thompson. An invaluable study of carriers and grounds, binding media, pigments, metals used in painting, al fresco and al secco techniques, burnishing, etc. used by the medieval masters. Preface by Bernard Berenson. 239pp. 5⅜ x 8.

T327 Paperbound $1.85

HANDBOOK OF ORNAMENT, F. S. Meyer. One of the largest collections of copyright-free traditional art: over 3300 line cuts of Greek, Roman, Medieval, Renaissance, Baroque, 18th and 19th century art motifs (tracery, geometric elements, flower and animal motifs, etc.) and decorated objects (chairs, thrones, weapons, vases, jewelry, armor, etc.). Full text. 300 plates. 3300 illustrations. 562pp. 5⅜ x 8.　　　　T302 Paperbound $2.50

Dover Books on Art

ART ANATOMY, Dr. William Rimmer. One of the few books on art anatomy that are themselves works of art, this is a faithful reproduction (rearranged for handy use) of the extremely rare masterpiece of the famous 19th century anatomist, sculptor, and art teacher. Beautiful, clear line drawings show every part of the body—bony structure, muscles, features, etc. Unusual are the sections on falling bodies, foreshortenings, muscles in tension, grotesque personalities, and Rimmer's remarkable interpretation of emotions and personalities as expressed by facial features. It will supplement every other book on art anatomy you are likely to have. Reproduced clearer than the lithographic original (which sells for $500 on up on the rare book market.) Over 1,200 illustrations. xiii + 153pp. 7¾ x 10¾.

T908 Paperbound $2.00

THE CRAFTSMAN'S HANDBOOK, Cennino Cennini. The finest English translation of IL LIBRO DELL' ARTE, the 15th century introduction to art technique that is both a mirror of Quatrocento life and a source of many useful but nearly forgotten facets of the painter's art. 4 illustrations. xxvii + 142pp. D. V. Thompson, translator. 5⅜ x 8.

T54 Paperbound $1.50

THE BROWN DECADES, Lewis Mumford. A picture of the "buried renaissance" of the post-Civil War period, and the founding of modern architecture (Sullivan, Richardson, Root, Roebling), landscape development (Marsh, Olmstead, Eliot), and the graphic arts (Homer, Eakins, Ryder). 2nd revised, enlarged edition. Bibliography. 12 illustrations. xiv + 266 pp. 5⅜ x 8.

T200 Paperbound $1.75

THE HUMAN FIGURE, J. H. Vanderpoel. Not just a picture book, but a complete course by a famous figure artist. Extensive text, illustrated by 430 pencil and charcoal drawings of both male and female anatomy. 2nd enlarged edition. Foreword. 430 illus. 143pp. 6⅛ x 9¼.

T432 Paperbound $1.45

PINE FURNITURE OF EARLY NEW ENGLAND, R. H. Kettell. Over 400 illustrations, over 50 working drawings of early New England chairs, benches, beds, cupboards, mirrors, shelves, tables, other furniture esteemed for simple beauty and character. "Rich store of illustrations . . . emphasizes the individuality and varied design," ANTIQUES. 413 illustrations, 55 working drawings. 475pp. 8 x 10¾.

T145 Clothbound $10.00

Dover Books on Art

HAWTHORNE ON PAINTING. Vivid re-creation, from students' notes, of instructions by Charles Hawthorne at Cape Cod School of Art. Essays, epigrammatic comments on color, form, seeing, techniques, etc. "Excellent," Time. 100pp. 5⅜ x 8.
T653 Paperbound $1.00

THE HANDBOOK OF PLANT AND FLORAL ORNAMENT, *R. G. Hatton.* 1200 line illustrations, from medieval, Renaissance herbals, of flowering or fruiting plants: garden flowers, wild flowers, medicinal plants, poisons, industrial plants, etc. A unique compilation that probably could not be matched in any library in the world. Formerly"The Craftsman's Plant-Book." Also full text on uses, history as ornament, etc. 548pp. 6⅛ x 9¼.
T649 Paperbound $3.00

DECORATIVE ALPHABETS AND INITIALS, Alexander Nesbitt. 91 complete alphabets, over 3900 ornamental initials, from Middle Ages, Renaissance printing, baroque, rococo, and modern sources. Individual items copyright free, for use in commercial art, crafts, design, packaging, etc. 123 full-page plates. 3924 initials. 129pp. 7¾ x 10¾.   T544 Paperbound $2.25

METHODS AND MATERIALS OF THE GREAT SCHOOLS AND MASTERS, Sir Charles Eastlake. (Formerly titled "Materials for a History of Oil Painting.") Vast, authentic reconstruction of secret techniques of the masters, recreated from ancient manuscripts, contemporary accounts, analysis of paintings, etc. Oils, fresco, tempera, varnishes, encaustics. Both Flemish and Italian schools, also British and French. One of great works for art historians, critics; inexhaustible mine of suggestions, information for practicing artists. Total of 1025pp. 5⅜ x 8.
Two volume set, T718-9 Paperbound $4.50

BYZANTINE ART AND ARCHAEOLOGY, O. M. Dalton. Still most thorough work in English on Byzantine art forms throughout ancient and medieval world. Analyzes hundreds of pieces, covers sculpture, painting, mosaic, jewelry, textiles, architecture, etc. Historical development; specific examples; iconology and ideas; symbolism. A treasure-trove of material about one of most important art traditions, will supplement and expand any other book in area. Bibliography of over 2500 items. 457 illustrations. 747pp. 6⅛ x 9¼.   T776 Clothbound $8.50

Dover Books on Art

FOOT-HIGH LETTERS: A GUIDE TO LETTERING, M. Price.
28 15½ x 22½" plates, give classic Roman alphabet, one foot
high per letter, plus 9 other 2" high letter forms for each letter.
16 page syllabus. Ideal for lettering classes, home study. 28 plates
in box.   T239 $6.00

A HANDBOOK OF WEAVES, G. H. Oelsner. Most complete
book of weaves, fully explained, differentiated, illustrated. Plain
weaves, irregular, double-stitched, filling satins; derivative,
basket, rib weaves; steep, broken, herringbone, twills, lace, tricot,
many others. Translated, revised by S. S. Dale; supplement on
analysis of weaves. Bible for all handweavers. 1875 illustrations.
410pp. 6⅛ x 9¼.   T209 Clothbound $5.00

*JAPANESE HOMES AND THEIR SURROUNDINGS, E. S.
Morse.* Classic describes, analyses, illustrates all aspects of traditional Japanese home, from plan and structure to appoint-
ments, furniture, etc. Published in 1886, before Japanese architecture was contaminated by Western, this is strikingly modern
in beautiful, functional approach to living. Indispensable to every
architect, interior decorator, designer. 307 illustrations. Glossary.
410pp. 5⅝ x 8⅜.   T746 Paperbound $2.25

THE DRAWINGS OF HEINRICH KLEY. Uncut publication of
long-sought-after sketchbooks of satiric, ironic iconoclast. Remarkable fantasy, weird symbolism, brilliant technique make
Kley a shocking experience to layman, endless source of ideas,
techniques for artist. 200 drawings, original size, captions translated. Introduction. 136pp. 6 x 9.   T24 Paperbound $1.65

COSTUMES OF THE ANCIENTS, Thomas Hope. Beautiful,
clear, sharp line drawings of Greek and Roman figures in full
costume, by noted artist and antiquary of early 19th century.
Dress, armor, divinities, masks, etc. Invaluable sourcebook for
costumers, designers, first-rate picture file for illustrators, commercial artists. Introductory text by Hope. 300 plates. 6 x 9.
                                             T21 Paperbound $2.00

VITRUVIUS: TEN BOOKS ON ARCHITECTURE. The most
influential book in the history of architecture. 1st century A.D.
Roman classic has influenced such men as Bramante, Palladio,
Michelangelo, up to present. Classic principles of design, har-
mony, etc. Fascinating reading. Definitive English translation by
Professor H. Morgan, Harvard. 344pp. 5⅜ x 8.
                                             T645 Paperbound $2.00

Dover Books on Art

HANDBOOK OF DESIGNS AND DEVICES, C. P. Hornung. A remarkable working collection of 1836 basic designs and variations, all copyright-free. Variations of circle, line, cross, diamond, swastika, star, scroll, shield, many more. Notes on symbolism. "A necessity to every designer who would be original without having to labor heavily," ARTIST AND ADVERTISER. 204 plates. 240pp. 5⅜ x 8.   T125 Paperbound $2.00

THE UNIVERSAL PENMAN, George Bickham. Exact reproduction of beautiful 18th-century book of handwriting. 22 complete alphabets in finest English roundhand, other scripts, over 2000 elaborate flourishes, 122 calligraphic illustrations, etc. Material is copyright-free. "An essential part of any art library, and a book of permanent value," AMERICAN ARTIST. 212 plates. 224pp. 9 x 13¾.   T20 Clothbound $10.00

AN ATLAS OF ANATOMY FOR ARTISTS, F. Schider. This standard work contains 189 full-page plates, more than 647 illustrations of all aspects of the human skeleton, musculature, cutaway portions of the body, each part of the anatomy, hand forms, eyelids, breasts, location of muscles under the flesh, etc. 59 plates illustrate how Michelangelo, da Vinci, Goya, 15 others, drew human anatomy. New 3rd edition enlarged by 52 new illustrations by Cloquet, Barcsay. "The standard reference tool," AMERICAN LIBRARY ASSOCIATION. "Excellent," AMERICAN ARTIST. 189 plates, 647 illustrations. xxvi + 192pp. 7⅞ x 10⅝.   T241 Clothbound $6.00

AN ATLAS OF ANIMAL ANATOMY FOR ARTISTS, W. Ellenberger, H. Baum, H. Dittrich. The largest, richest animal anatomy for artists in English. Form, musculature, tendons, bone structure, expression, detailed cross sections of head, other features, of the horse, lion, dog, cat, deer, seal, kangaroo, cow, bull, goat, monkey, hare, many other animals. "Highly recommended," DESIGN. Second, revised, enlarged edition with new plates from Cuvier, Stubbs, etc. 288 illustrations. 153pp. 11⅜ x 9.
                 T82 Clothbound $6.00

VASARI ON TECHNIQUE, G. Vasari. Pupil of Michelangelo, outstanding biographer of Renaissance artists reveals technical methods of his day. Marble, bronze, fresco painting, mosaics, engraving, stained glass, rustic ware, etc. Only English translation, extensively annotated by G. Baldwin Brown. 18 plates. 342pp. 5⅜ x 8.   T717 Paperbound $2.00

Dover Books on Art

THE COMPLETE BOOK OF SILK SCREEN PRINTING PRO-DUCTION, J. I. Biegeleisen. Here is a clear and complete picture of every aspect of silk screen technique and press operation—from individually operated manual presses to modern automatic ones. Unsurpassed as a guidebook for setting up shop, making shop operation more efficient, finding out about latest methods and equipment; or as a textbook for use in teaching, studying, or learning all aspects of the profession. 124 figures. Index. Bibliography. List of Supply Sources. xi + 253pp. 5⅜ x 8½.

T1100 Paperbound $2.00

A HISTORY OF COSTUME, Carl Köhler. The most reliable and authentic account of the development of dress from ancient times through the 19th century. Based on actual pieces of clothing that have survived, using paintings, statues and other reproductions only where originals no longer exist. Hundreds of illustrations, including detailed patterns for many articles. Highly useful for theatre and movie directors, fashion designers, illustrators, teachers. Edited and augmented by Emma von Sichart. Translated by Alexander K. Dallas. 594 illustrations. 464pp. 5⅛ x 7⅛.

T1030 Paperbound $2.75

CHINESE HOUSEHOLD FURNITURE, G. N. Kates. A summary of virtually everything that is known about authentic Chinese furniture before it was contaminated by the influence of the West. The text covers history of styles, materials used, principles of design and craftsmanship, and furniture arrangement—all fully illustrated. xiii + 190pp. 5⅝ x 8½.

T958 Paperbound $1.50

THE COMPLETE WOODCUTS OF ALBRECHT DURER, edited by Dr. Willi Kurth. Albrecht Dürer was a master in various media, but it was in woodcut design that his creative genius reached its highest expression. Here are all of his extant woodcuts, a collection of over 300 great works, many of which are not available elsewhere. An indispensable work for the art historian and critic and all art lovers. 346 plates. Index. 285pp. 8½ x 12¼.

T1097 Paperbound $2.50

Dover publishes books on commercial art, art history, crafts, design, art classics; also books on music, literature, science, mathematics, puzzles and entertainments, chess, engineering, biology, philosophy, psychology, languages, history, and other fields. For free circulars write to Dept. DA, Dover Publications, Inc., 180 Varick St., New York, N.Y. 10014.